It has always be___ to offer forgiveness and su___ ___en who are suffering—and that ___ ___uals. *Strangers in a Christian Land* helps ___ ___ith compassion at those trapped in a lifestyle n___y of us have long preferred to reject or ignore. Now, particularly with the deadly threat of AIDS all around us, the Church is called to face a great challenge. The pages that follow show how to meet that challenge and help homosexuals on the long and difficult road to wholeness.

"This book is an excellent introduction to the complex issues facing parents and spouses of homosexuals. I pray it will be a great help and blessing to thousands of loved ones!"

Bob Davies, Executive Director
Exodus International, San Rafael, California

"A practical resource for professional and lay counselors within the church.... In addition, it gives invaluable insights to the individuals struggling to leave the homosexual life."

Barbara Johnson, Director
Spatula Ministries, La Habra, California

"It is time the Christian community wakes up to the truth of homosexuality in families and in the Church. It is past time Christians got involved in being image-bearers of Jesus in crisis ministry. Darlene Bogle, with great sensitivity, truth and research, has written a healing account of the Christian position and the healing power of Christ. I recommend her book to everyone willing to face this reality."

Joanne Wallace
Internationally known speaker and author
Fremont, California

"Darlene Bogle turns the sex theories of men and women into cheesecloth by demonstrating in her life that the New Testament will do what it says it will do."

Sherwood Eliot Wirt
Editor emeritus, **Decision**

"What the world needs now is love, sweet love. Darlene Bogle found it not where she thought it was but rather in the service of the One whose yoke is easy and whose burden is light. The circumstances of her deliverance from what the Bible calls 'the pleasures of sin' are dramatic and victorious. I rejoice with my friend and thank God for her courage in telling about it in this gripping autobiography."

Norman B. Rohrer
Director, Christian Writer's Guild

Strangers In A Christian Land

Darlene Bogle

Published by
√ chosen books

FLEMING H. REVELL COMPANY
OLD TAPPAN, NEW JERSEY

Names and locations in this book have been changed to protect individual privacy.

All Scripture quotations in this book are from the Holy Bible, New International Version, copyright © 1973, 1978, 1984 International Bible Society. Used by permission of Zondervan Bible Publishers.

Library of Congress Cataloging-in-Publication Data

Bogle, Darlene.
    Strangers in a Christian land / Darlene Bogle.
    192 p.   cm. 21
    Includes bibliographical references.
    ISBN 0-8007-9160-6
    1. Church work with gays—United States.
    2. Homosexuality—Religious aspects—Christianity.   I. Title.
BV4437.5.B64   1990
261.8'35766—dc20   89-49577
                                                              CIP

A Chosen Book
Copyright © 1990 by Darlene Bogle

Chosen Books are published by
Fleming H. Revell Company
Old Tappan, New Jersey
Printed in the United States of America

To my mother, Faie Swanson,
now at home with Jesus.
Together, we learned
what "family" really means.
Thanks, Mom.

Acknowledgments

To the family and friends who have prayed and encouraged me in the writing of this book: Thank you.

To my church family at Hayward Foursquare Church who have reached out in love to me and those who seek healing through Paraklete Ministries: Thank you.

To the hundreds of people who have called or written to me with questions along their journey: Thank you for letting me be a part of your healing.

To the ministries of Exodus International: Thank you for your encouragement as we stand together to make a united statement for complete healing for those who struggle with homosexuality.

To Bonnie Wheeler, Dorothy Holmes and Don and Barbara Murray for reading and making constructive suggestions.

To Jane Campbell and Ann McMath for their editorial direction, and commitment to a vision of ministry outreach to the Church . . . and those who hurt.

To those who have not yet become committed to the journey of healing but will someday look for answers. . . . This book is dedicated especially to you.

Contents

Strangers In A Christian Land

1

When Gay Is Not Happy

More than a decade had passed since my life had taken its major turn toward wholeness, but inside my heart remained a haunting fear of rejection. I was visiting a friend whose children had known me only as Aunt Darlene. No mention had been made of my former homosexual lifestyle, because it simply did not matter.

Now it mattered: Laura's oldest daughter was entering high school, I was making frequent appearances on nationwide television and had a newly published book at the local Christian bookstore. The time had come to share my story.

My stomach was in knots. "I want to be the one to tell Theresa about my background," I confided to my friend Laura, "but I'm afraid she'll reject me."

Laura nodded. "Theresa's known you only as a Christian. Rejection is a chance you'll have to take." She paused. "But it's time to tell her. Theresa reads a lot, and I know she'd be hurt if she found out some other way."

I cleared a nervous tickle from my throat. "It's easier to appear on nationwide television and share my testimony than to stand face-to-face with one teenager I really love."

Laura slipped her arm around my shoulder. "Darlene, you've known a lot of hurt and rejection in your life. You need to trust in God's timing and His ability to bring understanding into Theresa's heart. Let's ask her to take a walk around the block with us."

My insides knotted with tension, and as the three of us walked my mind whirled with a hundred beginnings. I gulped to swallow the tight lump in my throat.

"Theresa—" I searched for the right words. "Have you ever wondered why I never married?"

She giggled. "I guess you never found the right man."

"Well, not exactly. . . ." I hesitated.

Laura interjected abruptly. "Theresa, you're old enough now to be told about Darlene's background. You know she's written a book."

"Yeah." Theresa looked puzzled.

"And you know that I told you to wait until you were older before you read it." She paused. "Did you ever wonder why?"

"Sure, but I figured it had to do with bad language or something."

I watched the cracks in the pavement as we walked, relieved that Laura had taken over the conversation.

"It wasn't the language. When Darlene was a child she was sexually abused by her father before she was a year old. Throughout her childhood, other men molested her. She was defenseless and formed a tough emotional shell to protect herself. She never learned to give or receive love as a child because her home life was one of neglect rather than nurturing."

I watched Theresa's face for a response as the words sank in. *Will she hate me when she hears the truth?* My heart raced, my face flushed with embarrassment.

"When Darlene was nine years old," Laura continued, "she was raped by a neighbor boy. At thirteen—your age—she was raped by a high school boy, and at eighteen she was raped at knifepoint by a man who offered her a ride home."

Theresa's face paled. Tears brimmed her eyelids, threatening to spill over.

"Darlene, you tell the rest."

I took a deep breath and scuffed my blue tennis shoes against the pavement. "All my life I felt empty, looking for love to fill the void. I thought that sexual intimacy could take away the pain. Men had hurt me, rejected me and victimized me. When I was seventeen, I met a girl who loved me. I made a choice that day to fill my emptiness with lesbian relationships."

I stopped walking and faced her, lifting my eyes to meet her gaze. "Theresa, I lived a homosexual lifestyle for the next seventeen years."

Her brow furrowed. "You're not now, are you?" She looked first at her mother, then back at me.

I laughed out of pure nervousness. "No. I'm not now. Several years ago God set me free from that lifestyle and began to show me how *He* could meet the need for intimacy that I'd been searching for all my life."

Theresa threw her arms around my neck, her shoulders

convulsing with deep sobs. Her tears soaked through my pink cotton blouse.

I wrapped my arms around her, mixing my tears with hers. Time seemed to stop for a moment on that busy street corner as we three embraced and wept in a moment of transparency and bonding.

Laura whispered the words I dared not vocalize. "Theresa, does this change how you feel about Darlene?"

"No," she sobbed. "It changes how I feel about *them!*"

The goal of this book is to do exactly that, to change how we feel about *them*. To show family and friends how to respond in a healing way to those loved ones, those seeming "strangers" caught in homosexuality or diagnosed with AIDS as a result of homosexual behavior.

With close-up profiles that reveal why they chose the label, the following pages will introduce you to people who have struggled with all kinds of temptations and have found healing for their sexual brokenness through a relationship with Jesus Christ. I know it is possible to become totally free from the homosexual struggle because I have experienced this freedom personally. Additionally, for the past ten years I have ministered to others who have moved into this wholeness.

Many who struggle with homosexuality have been raised in Christian homes. We will learn from some of them how Christ's freedom came—not in knowing the Scriptures, but in living them out daily.

Beyond the Gay Label

We tend to lump everyone who chooses homosexual behavior into a narrow category. Often we look at the label and decide it is the sum of the person. In order to offer total healing, however, it is important for us to understand that the events that caused someone to identify himself or herself as homosexual vary from person to person.

Thus, treating each person as an individual is an important first step to their healing. Although we recognize Jesus Christ as the source of all healing, understanding the individual experience of your friend or loved one is the best way to help him or her turn toward that healing Presence.

Jeff is an example of the reality that individuals involved in homosexual behavior can come from very different backgrounds—in this case, Christian.

Jeff, the son of missionaries. Since his parents were overseas most of his childhood and teenage years, he spent those years at a foreign mission school.

The first year away, an older boy in the dorm molested him. He was afraid to tell anyone and the abuse continued for an entire year.

Jeff returned to the States to attend a Christian college, where he was again seduced into a homosexual encounter. Then he began living a double life, hoping his parents would never find out, but he was eventually kicked out of school for drinking.

Years later Jeff returned to his childhood faith through the testimony of an ex-gay. Then he went to his parents and confessed the entire story of his early abuse and the ensuing sin that had separated him from them and from God for many years. Jeff had begun the long journey to wholeness. Now he is committed to living out his faith and finding complete freedom from the brokenness of sexual abuse and homosexuality.

Just as we cannot assume that all homosexuals fit neatly into a package, so we cannot always understand why one son or daughter chooses a homosexual lifestyle while the other children do not. A very high percentage of the women and men I counsel have been victims of incest, rape or other sexual abuse as children. This is one starting place in pursuing healing. Many times the victimization occurred so long ago that the memories are submerged. In cases of sexual abuse I recommend consultation with trained Christian professionals to facilitate healing.

In some cases, the person has come from an alcoholic family structure and grew up with dysfunctional role-modeling. For him or her, a local support group for adult children of alcoholics might be an important resource.

While we as family and friends need to look beyond the gay label when confronting homosexual involvement, we should encourage the Church to do the same. Jesus Christ is the only One who can provide the power to change a life. But though the saving power of Jesus is the message of the Church, the Body of Christ has not always been quick to offer spiritual support to homosexuals seeking to build or rebuild their relationship with Jesus.

Such was the case with Lynn. The daughter of a minister, Lynn knew well the Bible teaching on homosexuality. Yet, as a college freshman, she chose to move to another state to live out the feelings she had struggled with for years. When she left, she told her parents she was choosing homosexuality over Christianity because she felt more supported and loved by the gay community than by Christians.

Her mother was devastated and wept for weeks, unable to share her pain with anyone in the church. Lynn's father took a harder view. "When you decide to put God first in your life," he told her, "you are welcome to come home. Until then, don't bother to darken the door of this home, or my church."

Lynn returned to her hometown several times. Her mother would sneak away and spend a few hours with her; her father refused to speak to her. Lynn was never allowed to visit the family home. Naturally, people in the church suspected the truth.

Through almost twenty years of struggle, she met Christians who condemned homosexuality, yet said they loved the homosexual. Lynn was locked into the rejection of her father, however, and could never quite believe anyone could love her in her homosexual struggle.

Then her life changed. She went to work in a new office complex and met a co-worker within days who had recently committed his life to Christ. She thought he was somewhat effeminate and questioned him about being gay.

"I used to be," he told her, "but now I'm finding out God's intent for my life—and my sexuality. I go to an ex-gay support group. The men and women are all Christians and all former gays. Would you like to come with me some evening?"

She thought about it and agreed to attend a meeting. At the group she found Christians who did accept her, and convinced her through Scripture that God loved her, too, and wanted to heal her brokenness.

Lynn is now active in leadership in an ex-gay ministry and is a functioning part of the Body of Christ. Sadly, the process of restoration with her family and her father's church is not easy, though she is working to rebuild those relationships. The pathway to healing is long, and difficult at best.

Lynn's story is no exception. Many times rejection comes from the family unit, and all too often it comes from church leaders who do not know how to bring healing to the homosexual struggler, especially since there is no shortage of examples in which change does not happen.

One mother from New York contacted me when her son challenged her to find someone, somewhere, who had been gay and was now living for Christ.

She had been looking for several months when she found my book at a Christian bookstore and called me. I was able to put her in touch with a ministry closer to her home. She gave the information to her son, and now we are both praying he will make the contact and find renewed hope for the possibility of change.

The response of the Church may range from harsh condemnation in some fundamentalist groups to the open acceptance of a group like the Metropolitan Community Church. M.C.C. was founded by the Rev. Troy Perry in 1968 as a support to gay men and lesbians who did not want to change their lifestyle but wanted God's sanction on their behavior. M.C.C. teaches that homosexuality is a gift of God and He is not concerned whom you sleep with. Perry does not identify homosexuality as sin, and the denomination has developed a polished response, complete with Scriptures they say prove that homosexuality is a union approved by God. (M.C.C. has applied for several years for acceptance into the National Council of Churches but had not gained entry as of spring 1990).

An orthodox Christian viewpoint on homosexuality should be balanced with the teaching of the entire Word of

God. There is no sin or sinner beyond God's ability to redeem. The balance comes in addressing this issue as the Bible does, calling it sin, then acknowledging God's enabling for victory over that sin.

Many men and women, our own sons and daughters, brothers and sisters, agonize silently before a God who they are not even sure loves them. They might not take on the public label of gay or even admit their struggle, but they are well-acquainted with the pull of same-sex attraction.

This is true within the Church family. Unsure of the Church's response, many keep silent about their struggles and go on to become elders, Sunday school teachers, even ministers, without resolving their inner conflicts. The evangelical Christian's struggle seldom goes away; it just gets buried deeper, waiting to erupt.

Richard called me from the Midwest. He had read one of my articles in a national magazine and saw the reference to *Long Road to Love*. He purchased the book from the next town where no one would know him, took the book home and began to read.

Suddenly it occurred to him that as the head deacon in his church, he was to host the next board meeting in his home. Richard felt compelled to hide the book and magazine so no one would see the titles and get suspicious. He took both publications, placed them in a zip-lock bag and dropped them into his deep freezer.

Great fear kept Richard from seeking healing in his own church. But after reading my story he felt he could talk to a stranger about a problem that had plagued him more than twenty years. I put him in contact with a ministry in his state that could offer help and support and keep his identity confidential.

I have received many calls over the past few years from men and women like Richard. Established in a church, they have no one to share their struggle with. They represent all groups: teenagers, young adults, marrieds, singles, church workers, missionaries, writers, sometimes even ministry leaders.

Homosexuality can no longer be separated as an "us-and-them" problem, for it touches every Christian denomination and almost every family line.

Fortunately, though we have a long way to go, change is taking place. Some churches are realizing the desperate need and are beginning to face the problem. Other churches, while still unsure about their own roles in ministering to homosexuals, are willing to support organizations with the means and determination to reach out. Then, in turn, as the integrity of ex-gay ministries wins them acceptance, hundreds of churchgoers who have overcome their homosexual struggles stand to be counted. This formerly silent minority in evangelical circles is slowly finding a voice to proclaim freedom.

Ministries

As Christian families and the Church look for answers for their loved ones, they are finding resources for support and healing that have sprung up across the world. One of the most prominent, based in San Rafael, California, is Exodus International.

It is the strong principle of accountability that aided in the formation of Exodus International in 1976. Exodus, an organization that refers homosexuals and parents to ministries around the country, is highly successful. It seeks to equip and unify agencies and individuals to communicate effectively the message of liberation from homosexuality through repentance and faith in Jesus Christ as Savior and Lord. At the same time, guidelines for affiliation have been drawn up and ministries are accountable to the leaders over their areas in a system of spiritual checks and balances. This accountability contributes to the continued growth and maturity of the leaders and ensures the integrity of the ministries.

Exodus has become an international overseer and support, and a major resource for families and friends seeking information to help their loved ones. (For information on how to contact Exodus, see Appendix III.)

There is another side to the story of ex-gay ministries, however, that must be included here. Alongside the growing number of support groups is a growing number of folded ministries. Some fold for lack of financial support, but many are abandoned when the leaders fall back into sexual sin. Many times the cause of the fall was simply that the leader was not well-founded spiritually or had not matured enough to be in leadership.

One major ex-gay ministry was devastated when its mature, professional leader became involved in sexual encounters with several counselees. He had concealed the involvements for a number of years, but they were discovered eventually and lives were ruined. In addition, a light of suspicion was cast upon all ex-gay ministries.

And, of course, the gay community and pro-gay organizations exploit the story of one fallen leader as proof that "once gay, always gay." Any high-profile ex-homosexual leader is subject to attack in the gay press and must have a strong support of prayer from the church family.

This only underscores the importance of the message and ministry. Families and friends can reach out to homosexuals with the healing light of Jesus' love, and must continue to do so. Nothing else can help those caught in the emptiness of the gay lifestyle.

Although the M.C.C. says we should extend full acceptance to their lifestyle, Leanne Payne states in her book *The Broken Image:* " 'Love is something more stern and splendid than mere kindness,' as C.S. Lewis has said, and the most unloving thing I could possibly have done to [a woman counselee] would have been to substitute some sort of mindless 'loving acceptance' for the very things that were killing her."

When gay is no longer happy, we can offer the hope of a God who heals and renews, the tenacity of family and friends who won't give up, the message of growing ex-gay ministries proclaiming the possibility of change, and the support of a loving Church that can learn to meet the needs of the homosexual struggler.

Let's take a closer look now at the causes of homosexuality and some of the arguments, from inside and outside the Church, regarding the possibility for change.

2

Such Were Some of You

A greasy spoon restaurant sandwiched between a large department store and a 24-hour supermarket in the heart of Los Angeles was the location for our counseling session. I was meeting with Beverly, a confirmed lesbian of more than forty years. Our conversation was almost drowned out by yells from the short-order cook and the clatter of silverware and dishes as the waitress cleared the booths.

Beverly stared at me intently, her green eyes revealing the hardness of her lesbian lifestyle. She puffed nervously on her Winston.

"I had to see you in person," she said. "I could only tell if you were for real if I saw you. I need to hear you say there is hope for change . . . even for me."

I met her gaze. "God is no respecter of persons. He released me from lesbianism after seventeen years and He'll do the same for you."

Over the next few hours, coffee refills and a growing pile of cigarette butts proclaimed a silent monument to her confusion and anxiety as Beverly told me her story. She had tried to go straight seven years earlier and met with one frustration after another. She had even started attending a well-known church and after several weeks made an appointment with the pastor, looking for specific ministry to help with the struggle, the inner isolation and loneliness, and for assurance that there was a way out of the lifestyle that gripped her life.

The words still carried venom as she relayed to me what the pastor had said: "I don't know how to help your kind; I'm not sure there is any help for you. And what's more, I'm not sure God even wants you people in church."

Beverly's eyes brimmed now with tears. She had walked out of the church that day and away from all forms of Christianity. But as I talked with her I learned she had not been able to kill a seed of hope that had been planted years before by her mother, a seed that said, "All that the Father gives me will come to me, and whoever comes to me I will never drive away" (John 6:37). The seed was there, and that day she was asking for water to help it grow.

I wish I could say this story is the exception, that everyone who goes to his or her pastor finds warmth, acceptance and encouragement to change. That is not yet the case.

One young man told me, "I talked to my pastor once. He told me to quit masturbating and not to think about men. I never went back for help, because I couldn't let him know that stopping the acts didn't stop the war inside me. I was still gay, even if I lived in self-imposed isolation."

A response of openness and help for the homosexual, in

other words, is not always easy to find. Those of us who want to help need to offer a biblical response. Can a homosexual change, or is he or she locked into that lifestyle with no alternative possible?

Let's start by looking at some suggested causes of homosexuality.

Scientific Studies

Today, it seems, everyone is prepared to offer a theory on what causes homosexuality, and what, if anything, can change that orientation. As scientific researchers try to understand genetic predisposition, secular psychologists concentrate on environment and early childhood role modeling. Generally, Christian therapists discount hormonal imbalances and suggest that individual responsibility to biblical standards can bring healing regardless of any other factors, such as childhood experiences.

The importance of the origin of homosexuality is pivotal, since homosexuals often argue, "I was born this way. I can't change." Were they?

The pioneer of the scientific study of homosexuality early in this century was Havelock Ellis with his work *Sexual Inversion*. He advanced the theory that homosexual behavior was the result of genetic and biological factors rather than psychological experiences.

In a recent study of Ellis' work, reported in Judd Morman's book *Homosexual Behavior*, Garfield Tourney traced the changing attitudes of scientists and psychologists from that original position to theories of endocrine imbalance (Forel, 1924) and early conditioning (Kinsey, Pomeroy and Martin, 1948).

A study by William Perloff, M.D. (1965), pointed out the lack of evidence to support the theory of hormonal factors as a cause of homosexuality and led Tourney to conclude that hormonal disturbances were not evident in homosexual subjects.

Perloff, while chief of the Division of Endocrinology and Reproduction at Einstein Medical Center in Philadelphia, conducted studies confirming that estrogens (steroid hormones promoting female characteristics) administered to normal men decreased their libido, but in no sense altered their sexual orientation. Perloff found that the administration of large doses of androgen (steroid hormones promoting male characteristics) to normal women may have intensified their sexual desires, but did not cause them to assume male roles.

Genetic research has since tried to substantiate a theory that insufficient androgen in the fetus will produce a male with female characteristics, thus supporting a "born homosexual" position. While insufficient amounts of androgen will produce changes in the fetus, homosexuality has not been proven to be attributed to pre-birth conditions.

In 1971 tests were conducted with a control group of lesbians. The studies indicated that abnormalities in the endocrine function, along with psychological factors, may be significant in the genesis of homosexuality. This was one of the few studies on female homosexuality in which all the subjects—although only four took part in the test—demonstrated a gross distortion of the pattern of testosterone, estrogen and luteinizing hormone output. The findings, described in Morman's *Homosexual Behavior*, are interpreted as possibly reflecting the infringement of psychological factors upon the hypothalamus.

Tourney further states that, at present, while one cannot dismiss the role of hormonal mechanisms in some aspects of homosexuality, those investigations have proven only suggestive, not definitive. Instead, science seems to be determining more and more that children are born sexually neutral—neither heterosexual nor homosexual. Their gender is determined when they are born, but their identity is developed by environmental influences.

Psychological Factors

The environmental influence is gaining wide acceptance, as is evidenced by the work of research psychologist Dr. Elizabeth Moberly. Her compelling look at the healing of the homosexual identity is presented with detailed analysis in *Homosexuality: A New Christian Ethic* and *Psychogenesis: The Early Development of Gender Identity*. Both works are valuable resources for understanding how the condition of homosexuality develops.

Moberly holds that the homosexual has been unable to meet the normal developmental need for attachment to the parent of the same sex, and that this legitimate developmental need must be met before true healing can occur. In *Psychogenesis* she writes,

> A homosexual orientation does not depend on a genetic predisposition or hormonal imbalance or abnormal learning processes, but on difficulties in the parent/child relationship, especially in the early years. The homosexual, whether man or woman, has suffered some deficit in the relationship with the parent of the same sex and there is a corresponding drive to make good this deficit.

Moberly's studies, clinical and detailed, are opening new frontiers in the understanding of the homosexual condition.

Masters and Johnson in their 1984 study on human sexuality affirm that homosexuality is not inborn. They conclude, "The genetic theory of homosexuality has been generally discarded today. Despite the interest in possible hormone mechanism in the origin of homosexuality, no serious scientist today suggests that a simple cause and effect relationship applies."

Additionally, in their 1979 study *Homosexuality in Perspective* they write, "It is of vital importance that all professionals in the mental health field keep in mind that the homosexual man or woman is basically a man or woman by genetic determination and homosexually oriented by learned preference."

Some psychologists go even further and treat homosexuality as a disorder, regardless of the American Medical Association's declassification of homosexuality in 1973 from a mental illness to a "condition." Dr. Gerard van der Aardweg, a psychotherapist in the Netherlands for over twenty years and a Christian, wrote in his book *Homosexuality and Hope* that "in my opinion, anyone who tries to approach the available physiological and psychological research literature openmindedly will have to admit that the best-fitting interpretation of homosexuality must be the idea of a neurotic variant."

William Wilson, professor of psychiatry and research fellow in medicine at Duke University, states in his book *Answers to Your Questions About Homosexuality*,

> The experience of many investigators and therapists strongly indicates that homosexuality is caused by

disturbed parental relationships with the child and significant others in a nurturing environment. There is no evidence that genetic or hormonal factors play any role in the development of homosexuality.

If psychological factors—particularly bearing on small children—are a primary influence on sexual identity, then the child's home life and relationship with his or her parents are critical.

Childhood Parental Bonding

While input from both parents is important for the healthy development of a child, the father's seems to be the key influence. Females learn about their femininity from their fathers. It is important for girls to go through the Daddy's-little-girl stage and to be affirmed that they are pretty. They may imitate their mothers, but it is in pleasing their fathers that femininity is called forth.

Males, too, learn role identification from their fathers. While they learn masculinity from their mothers' affirmations, they need that special bonding with their dads to develop a vitally important security in their maleness.

Particularly interesting in view of today's growing society of single-parent homes is the advice of Christian psychologist W. Peter Blitchington in his book *Sex Roles and the Christian Family:*

A boy needs contact with his father in order for his sexual identity to be developed properly. Boys whose fathers are absent, passive or rejecting often find it harder to identify with the male role.

In relationship to girls, he explains:

> Since sexual behavior is first and most deeply learned
> in relationships with the opposite-sexed parent,
> many young girls are going to find themselves unable
> to handle an adult sexual and emotional relationship
> with a man if their own fathers were absent during
> the early part of their lives.

Blitchington defines male and female roles in a biblical
context as well as from a psychological and environmental
perspective. He believes there is no stronger method of
prevention for homosexuality than the healthy family unit
committed to Jesus Christ. That unit is not a one hundred
percent guarantee that homosexuality will not invade your
family, but it is the best preventive measure.

Another Christian psychologist, George Rekers, af-
firms in his book *Growing Up Straight* that the "best insurance against sexual deviation is a healthy family life."
His findings support Blitchington's that role modeling in
the early years plays a crucial part in a child's development.

While this is a significant aspect of prevention, many
parents are unaware of their child's involvement in homosexuality until later in his or her life. Then the issues must
be dealt with adult-to-adult, which is often more difficult.

Many parents tend to feel guilty that they didn't "do the
right things" as their child was growing up. Later in this
book (see chapter 7) we will deal with overcoming that
guilt and helping the child assume responsibility for his or
her choices. Part of assuming responsibility is a realistic
look at what the Scriptures have to say about homosexuality.

A major issue is whether homosexuality is unavoidable

or the result of choices that lead to involvement. As we have seen, scientific evidence suggests more and more that it is a chosen, not inherited, behavior. Even if it were inherited, however, even if science could prove that homosexuality is thrust on an infant in the womb, it could not offer hope to those who want to change.

This concept of the possibility of change is vital to Christians who must resolve the moral issue of homosexuality in a biblical manner. As we look to the Bible as the absolute standard of morality, so we look to its promise that with God nothing is impossible (see Jeremiah 32:17, 27). Given even the slightest possibility that He is able to help men and women redirect their behavioral responses and heal their broken sexual orientation, then homosexuality becomes a question of right and wrong.

Is Change Possible?

A good place to start a discussion of homosexuality and the freedom offered in Scripture is Romans 5:19: "For just as through the disobedience of the one man the many were made sinners, so also through the obedience of the one man the many will be made righteous."

Since the rebellion of Adam, every human being has entered this world with iniquity, the condition of and predisposition to sin. The form it embraces in each person may vary, but the bent to sin is etched into every soul. The Bible states clearly, moreover, that homosexuality is a particular sin. Romans 1 states that homosexuality is an abomination to God. First Corinthians 6 lists homosexuality with other sins from which we must turn in order to inherit the Kingdom of God.

Where mankind differs from other animals is that we can turn from sin; that we are created with a free will; that once regenerated by Jesus Christ, we can choose to say no to our lower nature and walk in the righteousness won by Jesus at Calvary.

In 2 Corinthians 5:17 we read, "Therefore, if anyone is in Christ, he is a new creation; the old has gone, the new has come!"

God would not act consistently with His own nature if He condemned what we could not help.

Hundreds of men and women today attest that they have been changed by the power of Jesus Christ and are no longer in bondage to homosexual desire.

Surely our God is more powerful than any sin, and any who believe they are somehow deficient can be assured that He who created the genetic balance is powerful enough to restore them to wholeness.

Let's look at that passage in 1 Corinthians:

> Do you not know that the wicked will not inherit the kingdom of God? Do not be deceived: Neither the sexually immoral nor idolaters nor adulterers nor male prostitutes *nor homosexual offenders* nor thieves nor the greedy nor drunkards nor slanderers nor swindlers will inherit the kingdom of God. And that is what some of you were. But you were washed, you were sanctified, you were justified in the name of the Lord Jesus Christ and by the Spirit of our God.
> 1 Corinthians 6:9–11

"And that is what some of you were. . . ." Past tense. It is possible biblically to change! Case studies may focus on the casualties of the Christian faith who have tried to change and failed. Studies may report that change is rare, if not impossible. But the Word of God says differently. We are cautioned in 2 Corinthians 10:12, "When [some] measure themselves by themselves and compare themselves with themselves, they are not wise."

As parents, family and friends, we need to change our focus from the behavior to God's promise of healing. We need to reach out to our loved ones with an unconditional message of hope.

One important question asked by those who want to minister to homosexuals has been, "Is there complete freedom from orientation, or must behavior be altered by white-knuckle endurance?"

Over the past few years, numerous books have hit the marketplace offering limited degrees of hope. Some proclaim that abstinence and frustrated celibacy are the primary expectation. One leading family counselor points out that breaking the habits of homosexuality will not guarantee that the individual will become heterosexual. And some state outright that heterosexuality is not an option for someone who has been a confirmed homosexual.

While it is true that ceasing the acts of homosexuality will not make someone a heterosexual, I believe strongly, by the evidence of Scripture and the power of God and the testimony of many, that healing and restoration to heterosexuality are available to homosexuals who will turn from their lifestyles to follow Christ.

Jesus said in John 8:31–32, "If you hold to my teaching, you are really my disciples. Then you will know the truth, and the truth will set you free." Again in John 14:6 He said, "I am the way and the truth and the life."

To be sure, there is enough power in the name of Jesus, the Person of Jesus and the blood of Calvary to transform anyone who comes to Him seeking a life change.

Jesus does not leave us half-delivered from the influence of Satan. He doesn't play spiritual roulette, setting some free and leaving others in bondage. He proclaimed His message of hope repeatedly throughout Scripture: Whoever came to Him would never be turned away. Today He still provides the power to live a life of self-control and responsible behavior to all willing to let Him be Lord of their lives.

The debates about homosexual behavior will continue as long as men and women seek to justify behavior contrary to God's law. If we had only one verse upon which to hang our belief in the possibility of change, however, we would not need to look beyond 1 Corinthians 6:11: "Such *were* some of you . . ." (KJV).

Oh, yes. Beverly, my lesbian acquaintance with more than forty years of homosexual involvement? The last time I heard from her she was settled in a small church with a compassionate pastor who believes deeply that change is possible. She is making choices not to go to gay bars and not to participate in activities with her former friends. She has changed her mode of dress to more feminine clothing, and says she feels clean for the first time in years. She took the seeds of hope and watered them with the Word of God . . . and change is growing in her life.

In many ways, Beverly's situation is rare. She didn't let the rejection of her family or hostile words from one minister turn her away from seeking healing. Given the testimony of just one life that has changed, she felt she could believe.

Our hearts should break for those who have quit looking.

3

Strangers in a Christian Land

The Bible is full of irony. In Exodus we read the story of the children of Israel who took forty years to make a trip that should have required two weeks.

They could have possessed their Promised Land, received their inheritance and shortened our reading material in the Old Testament!

Instead they grumbled, resisted leadership direction, failed to believe the promises of God and lived in rebellion.

The sin nature of our forefathers is alive and well, along with the sad irony that the depravity of mankind is evident even in evangelical churches. Those who struggle with homosexual feelings and have sought freedom can relate to the account from Exodus. Although the Promised Land was available, it seemed unattainable, and the children of Israel were a long time in claiming their inheritance.

Now a new inheritance has been declared from the cross of Calvary, a promised land that every one of us can enter to find freedom and wholeness. Every person who has struggled with homosexuality and has repented receives the same inheritance of freedom as every other forgiven sinner. The land of Christendom is supposed to be one of fellowship, acceptance, family living and a safe refuge from the perils of homosexual compulsions.

The inheritance promise is there, but many strangers from the desert of homosexuality find no land flowing with the milk and honey of Christian fellowship.

There are giants of deception, prejudice and fear that must be overcome.

Who Are the Strangers?

Those who struggle with feelings of homosexuality and believe they need help come from two major groups.

One group comprises unchurched persons who may or may not have had Christian training in their childhoods. They have been part of the gay community and have identified themselves openly as homosexuals. Then, through whatever set of circumstances God has brought into their lives, they have personal encounters with Jesus. They begin to identify with Him and respond to His call on their lives. They repent, want to change their behavior to be pleasing to God and realize this includes finding a church family where they can grow. They start to deal with issues in their lives that were only complicated by their homosexual involvements.

These are the "strangers" most likely to find groups such as those affiliated with Exodus International. These ex-gay support groups represent many homosexuals' initial contact with the Christian community. Often they have heard someone share a testimony of healing from sexual brokenness and are curious about the process. If they stay with it, they will learn how to work through the changes that will help them claim their inheritance of acceptance by the Church.

There are growing numbers of such persons who are now "coming out" and stating that change and healing are both viable realities made possible by Jesus Christ.

It is from evangelical churches that I find the second group of strangers who struggle with homosexuality. These are not vocal adherents but part of a silent minority. Christians who struggle with homosexual feelings, who have secret sexual encounters and guilt-ridden hearts, make up more than eighty percent of my counseling calls. They are ministers, missionaries, deacons, pastors' wives, Sunday school teachers and lay people from every denomination.

They are accepted in the Christian community because they know how others would respond if they confided their struggle, so they don't. Often they marry and have children. They give no hint of their tormented feelings. Often their struggle is entirely internal. They have never acted out their compulsions, yet they agonize over guilt.

Gay activists would encourage them to "come out," to declare what they "really are" inside, to act out their feelings. Their Christian faith tells them, however, that acting out homosexuality is not God's plan for their lives. Thus they repress their feelings, hoping someday for healing. When they do risk reaching out for help, it is to professional counselors who will respect confidentiality. They cannot chance losing their positions or their families.

Involvement in homosexual activity among church members is being highlighted more frequently due to the AIDS epidemic. A secret that could have been kept a lifetime is now exposed with the growing frequency of HIV-positive cases.

Jeffrey Collins, executive director of Love in Action, a Christian ministry of compassion to AIDS patients in the Washington, D.C., area, has helped reveal the scope of the struggle. Collins wrote in the 1988 Resolution on AIDS of the National Association of Evangelicals: "Among the more than 130 AIDS patients with whom we work are a former female impersonator at a Washington gay bar, an honors graduate of the U.S. Naval Academy, a Baptist minister, the former student body president of a major evangelical university, a choir director and several elders and deacons."

People, in short, like Adam. Adam was reared in a Christian home. He came from three generations of preachers, and his family expected him to carry on the ministry tradition.

Adam was a natural when it came to working with young people, and he spent his teenage years counseling at summer youth camps. No one suspected his struggles with homosexuality.

Throughout his teens and into early adulthood he was popular with girls, but he never dated any one girl very long. He went away to Bible school and graduated as an appointed evangelist in his denomination. He had a charismatic personality and was well-liked by both young and older church members.

As an evangelist, Adam filled his sermons with vivid imagery that would stir his hearers to fresh commitment to Christ. He quoted Scripture with ease, having memorized entire books from his youth. Still no one suspected his sexual orientation.

Adam ministered nationwide for almost fifteen years. Suddenly his ministry folded. His denomination revoked his credentials and his secret struggle became common knowledge. Adam was accused of homosexual conduct against several boys in a small town who had confessed the incidents to their pastor.

When confronted, Adam admitted to a lifelong struggle he had not been able to overcome. His ministry was shattered, along with the trust of his denomination. Further investigation produced the names of hundreds of young men he had seduced during those years he had ministered at youth camps.

After hearing about Adam and receiving many calls from Christian men and women caught in the vice of homosexuality, I began to ask myself why. Many of these people were involved in relationships with other Christians from their church families. Why and how, I wondered, does this sin seem to thrive in evangelical churches?

A Few Answers

In church, although we are taught to avoid the sins of the world, we let down our guards somehow when we are in a totally Christian environment. I have spoken with dozens of men and women who first got involved in homosexuality at Christian colleges

They felt somehow that the environment was safe and would protect them. Many times it only provided a release for the feelings they had repressed at home.

Also, even in Christian colleges, rebellion against leadership and rules is almost traditional. Little by little, encouraged by peer pressure, many students relax a standard and take a drink or smoke a joint. Sometimes they go as a group to bars in towns nearby and party through the weekend. Most never see the web of entrapment that Satan is skillfully weaving.

Third, what Adam and many others have learned the hard way is that you can never look to other people to meet those deep unmet needs from childhood that we discussed in the last chapter. If a relationship with Christ is not top priority, something else will be. It is not enough just to believe in God. It is not enough to know Scripture. It is not even enough to ask Christ to be your Savior. There is a relationship with Jesus that must be nurtured every day in order to prevent compensatory, dependent and sinful relationships with others.

Many Christian women I speak with tell of sensing a need for nurture somehow missing in their marriage relationship. It is not sexual desire, but often something that goes back to their childhoods when they missed bonding with their mothers. A woman may have a good friendship and a satisfying sexual relationship with her husband, but the closeness of a female friend meets a different need.

Let me hasten to say that women have the capacity to enjoy healthy Christian friendships. Few close relationships turn into lesbian affairs. God has gifted women with an ability to love, care for and nurture not only children and husbands, but people on all levels of friendship. The key to healthy relationships, however, is that a woman rely on God rather than another individual to meet the deepest voids in her life.

Most Christian women I speak with have entered homosexual relationships as adults. Their struggles were initiated in childhood but not acted upon until later.

Not so with the men who contact me.

The stories are endless of young men going to church camp and being molested by a counselor; or being part of a youth group and being molested by the youth minister; or, more painful yet, going to the pastor to talk about sexual feelings as they approach puberty, and being entangled in a homosexual encounter with the minister.

Frank Worthen of Love in Action, for instance, was a teenager when he went to his pastor to talk about confusing emotions he was experiencing. His pastor told Frank he was having those feelings because he was homosexual, and that he should experience them fully. The pastor encouraged him to experience gay sex. For the next 25 years Frank embraced the homosexual lifestyle and never looked to the church for help.

Michael was in his first year of Bible college when he was invited to spend the weekend at the home of a popular unmarried religion teacher. He accepted, and was introduced to a homosexual lifestyle. He wanted to be accepted, so he never told anyone. Eventually, when he was kicked out of the college, no one believed his stories about the professor.

At the annual conferences of Exodus International, ministry leaders from around the country share what God is doing in their areas. They come to be refreshed and challenged to make an impact on the homosexual community for Christ. I hear hundreds of stories from these men and women who often found their own first sexual experience in a Christian environment.

I continue to be stunned at the extent of homosexuality in the Church, how it can be as much of a problem *in* the Church as out. But it tells me that the Church is full of hurting people with unmet needs who struggle with every sin known to mankind.

Christianity is not a label attached to abstract beliefs, after all, but a life that is meant to be lived under the Lordship of Jesus Christ in the midst of struggle and brokenness. We don't disdain the Church or family because of sickness not yet healed. Instead, we call for commitment to greater holiness for church leaders and Christian families alike, that we might all be more like Christ.

The Return to Basic Truth

Many are discouraged by the accounts of homosexual behavior within the ranks of leadership within the Church, particularly when the people involved find it so hard to give up.

I had heard the excuse, and used it myself for many years, that it was next to impossible to find a true ex-gay. When I heard about someone who claimed to be free of homosexuality, I would follow up in a few months when, sure enough, he or she had usually returned to the lifestyle. I had tried to change at least three times myself during my seventeen-year involvement in homosexuality. I always ended up falling back into sin.

I had failed to understand that whereas I wanted to change just one aspect of my life, Christ intended to change all my behavior and heal the deep brokenness in my life that caused me to continue to make defeating choices. Only when I began to understand that Jesus Himself could enable me to resist temptations did I see my way out. I had to look to Him alone as my example of freedom, since human beings are subject to continuing failure.

I found I could choose not to believe the lie that I simply could not help myself, that I "had" to sin. I found in Scripture that my behavior was under my control, and that, being dead to sin, I could reject sin and choose righteousness.

God does not force us to change against our will, nor can Satan force us to sin against our will. It always comes back to personal responsibility.

In the middle of a struggle with our emotions that have been aroused by indulgent behavior, it may seem as though there is no choice other than to continue obeying those urgings. The good news of vital Christianity, on the other hand, is that we can change our behavior at any point, regardless of the intensity of our emotions. In the case of homosexual behavior, the power to change is available when we come to Jesus Christ and seek wholeheartedly to change.

But we must realize that our ability to change is activated by repentance. And repentance is not possible without acknowledging the forbidden action as sin.

This is an important understanding for the family and friends who wish to assist the homosexual in the healing process. To define homosexual behavior as anything less than sin is to relegate it to limited healing, as a category, not subject to the broadest stroke of God's grace.

The gay rights coalition would have the straight society

believe that homosexual behavior is a natural condition of a fair-sized segment of society, that there is no need for change.

This is the opinion of Troy Perry, founder of the Metropolitan Community Church. He stated at the 1985 national covention for the M.C.C. that "Christ died for my sin; He didn't die for my sexuality."

Many well-intentioned Christians have walked in the shadow of the M.C.C. and pro-gay movements in recent years by speaking out for more compassion toward the homosexual, especially the homosexual with AIDS, often siding with more liberal denominations in calls to love, not judge. They present God as all-accepting, with no requirements for changing sexual behavior.

Since 1972 when the United Church of Christ became the first major denomination to ordain a homosexual, toleration for the lifestyle has edged into other denominations as well. An article in the November 13, 1989, issue of *Time* magazine entitled "The Battle Over Gay Clergy" reported on the ecclesiastical battle over the acceptance of gay ministers and priests. The Episcopal, United Methodist and Presbyterian (U.S.A.) Churches, among others, continue to discuss their stances on homosexual behavior, while suggestions of accommodation horrify grassroots conservatives.

In the Roman Catholic Church, despite strong Vatican decrees against homosexual behavior, as many as twenty percent of priests may be gay, based on the polls cited in the article.

Some mainline groups advocate "covenant" relationships, meant to be celibate but nevertheless homosexual. (Within the M.C.C. these relationships are regarded as

47

marriages and are intended to be monogamous.) Those who espouse covenant relationships have concluded that homosexual orientation cannot be changed, so it is unfair to exclude these individuals from loving and caring relationships.

Another article in *Time*, "Should Gays Have Marriage Rights?" (November 20, 1989), relates that a "domestic partnership movement" is pushing for benefits for gay couples equivalent to those received by married couples. These include health plan coverage, inheritance rights and claims to rent-controlled apartments. According to the article, efforts are being made to change laws across the country—sometimes successfully—to offer legal benefits to homosexual partners. There is also a push to allow them to apply for a "certificate of domestic partnership" legalizing the relationship.

Many mainline churches, in choosing to ignore God's call to moral responsibility, have tried to redefine what specific sexual activities are being addressed in the Scriptures on homosexuality. They fail to acknowledge that regardless of a perceived orientation toward heterosexuality or homosexuality, God still requires sexual abstinence in the unmarried Christian. Since homosexual marriages or unions are not legal, not to mention unbiblical, they do not validate the acting out of homosexual behavior as an acceptable practice to God.

Contrary to Troy Perry's belief, Christ did die for our sexual redemption, when the expression of our sexuality is sinful behavior. The only acceptable standard of sexual responsibility must be what Scripture teaches, not what we feel about that teaching.

If we offer the homosexual healing from the behavior in

which he engages, without hope of changing the orientation that causes the behavior, we present an impotent Christ. Jesus died for our sin, all aspects of it. He came to make us whole persons. It is important for us to have a clear understanding of what God wants to do for the homosexual. Again, the Scriptures declare total transformation: "Therefore, if anyone is in Christ, he is a new creation; the old has gone, the new has come!" (2 Corinthians 5:17).

To allow compassion to arise without offering the possibility of total healing will only intensify the homosexual's sinful condition, and thwart a church's ability to minister healing grace to him or her.

The ability to choose, to exercise our free will, is a gift of God meant to honor Him. Answering His call to holiness will not always be easy, nor will it always feel good, but it will always be accompanied by the enabling of the Holy Spirit to overcome sin.

When the homosexual struggle is most difficult, Christian family and friends can say with assurance that God will bring healing as their loved ones stand firm upon biblical principles. With faithful and loving endurance we can point those who struggle to a firm foundational hope for transformation.

God's part has been established clearly in the Scriptures; our part is to live out the teachings each day.

The challenge is to learn in modern-day practicality what it means to be a new creature in Christ. This involves establishing healthy relationships that are Christ-centered. It means making daily choices to turn from behavior that will feed the thought life with memories of the past. It may mean changing certain kinds of reading material, or even choosing to drive a different way to work in order to avoid an old neighborhood.

Each choice will contribute to how quickly a person can cease to be a stranger in a Christian land and be called no more a servant of sin, but a friend of Jesus (John 15:15). No more a stranger, but a son or daughter receiving the inheritance of life.

4

Back to Basics

Families are often stunned to learn that a loved one is involved in a homosexual lifestyle. Once the shock has settled into resignation, they begin to ask a barrage of emotional questions: What can I do? Is there any help for him [or her]? How can I make him [or her] be normal again?

We will look at some elemental answers to these questions in this chapter. The approach to these answers, however, depends on one important factor: whether or not the person *wants* to change. This is something you must answer honestly if you have a loved one in this situation, because if he does not want to change you are, naturally, in a more difficult position.

Still, there is effective work to do. Let's look first at the basics for helping someone who wants to turn from homosexuality.

Help to Change

It may not surprise you to learn that the two most important steps for someone who wants to change his behavior are prayer and Bible study.

Don't be fooled by the apparent simplistic nature of this advice! There is nothing more vital your friend or loved one can do than use the basic tools God has given him.

Have him read the Bible, pray daily on his own and join a group Bible study or prayer fellowship. Encourage him to pursue these areas even if he does not feel they are doing any good. Persistence is what makes the difference between despair and wholeness.

Your friend may feel disappointed in God because He has failed to answer prayers according to a particular time schedule. We have all heard that if we are specific with God we can "claim" this verse: "Therefore I tell you, whatever you ask for in prayer, believe that you have received it, and it will be yours" (Mark 11:24).

Your friend may have found, however, that in the struggle to overcome homosexual behavior he or she has prayed, pleaded and promised never again to indulge . . . yet freedom is elusive. It becomes easy then to blame God for not upholding His end of the bargain and throw in the towel on holiness. Prayer, it seems, has not worked.

I struggled with this for seventeen years. I loved the Lord and wanted to serve Him, yet I could never shake the feeling of attraction to other women. I felt justified that if God did not take the sexual feelings away immediately, then I had no alternative other than to act on them.

I found some help in these verses: "It is for freedom that Christ has set us free. Stand firm, then, and do not let yourselves be burdened again by a yoke of slavery" (Galatians 5:1) and "No temptation has seized you except what is common to man. And God is faithful; he will not let you be tempted beyond what you can bear. But when you are tempted, he will also provide a way out so that you can stand up under it" (1 Corinthians 10:13). I could not find one verse, however, to support the notion that if I felt like acting on my sinful desires, I was free to do it.

So I continued to pore over the Gospels and underlined the promises of Christ for freedom from sin, for victory over the influences of Satan. I studied what it means to be "in Christ."

Once I knew what was available, I began to pray and ask God to make those Scriptures a reality in my life.

Then I chose to act on what the Word of God said rather than how I felt about what it said.

For me, prayer became a time of talking things over with God, instead of asking Him to take away the feelings and emotions that, expressed in a healthy way, are a part of life. I learned that I could acknowledge sexual feelings, but that I needed maturity, growth and healing in order to live with them responsibly before Him. Prayer afforded a time of intimacy for me to grow more in love with Jesus.

I remembered the times when Marie Hollowell, my college dean of women, would tuck her arm around my shoulder and we would stand close and pray. She would whisper her prayers to Jesus, and I felt as though He were standing right there with His arms enfolding the two of us. Those times of prayer strengthened the assurance in me that I was loved unconditionally.

As I came to understand even a little of how much Jesus loved me, I grew in confidence to stand firm against Satan.

Until then, I had not recognized my authority to resist the powers of evil that sought to destroy my life.

Until we understand that Jesus not only defeated Satan, but passed on all authority for us to use in His name, we will never get off the treadmill of failure. Only then can we enjoy victory over Satan as a personal experience.

Ronald and Joanne Highley of L.I.F.E. Ministry in New York City shared some excellent insights in their July 1989 newsletter on the issue of unanswered prayer. "God does not answer a prayer to remove the feelings or attractions," they wrote, "when they are only the 'foliage,' the visible part of the problem. We don't get rid of dandelions by mowing the lawn. Homosexuality's roots are buried emotions and sin. Yes, love needs that have not been met, but also sinful reactions to being hurt and rejected. Therefore, God in His wisdom wants to uproot the problem totally, so that we can walk in freedom.

"These things are not accomplished in a weekend," they added, "but through a process, liberty is found."

The new convert will often be looking at the Bible for the first time. It is fresh and alive, giving hope for a complete change of lifestyle. He or she understands the depravity of life without Christ, and hungers for wholeness.

New converts devour the gospels and the epistles, and find themselves falling in love with Jesus, Christians and the Church. Although there are giants to overcome, they believe for the first time that they can be freed from their homosexual struggle.

Christians who have heard the Gospel from childhood have a separate hurdle to overcome. They need to look afresh at the Bible as the road map for their lives and gain an expectation of how Jesus is going to work out His life in them. These Christians need to reread the Bible and ask the Holy Spirit to excite their expectations. Just reading the words is not sufficient.

Renae told me she had spent five years trying to overcome the inner pull that drew her constantly to lesbian relationships. She was a Christian, had resolved to leave her past behind and had cut off all relationships that would keep her connected to the gay world. She prayed for a Christian roommate so she would have someone to teach her about Christian friendship. The roommate was a long-time Christian, but turned out also to be attracted to lesbianism. Soon Renae had deeper emotional conflicts to resolve. She didn't feel safe anywhere, let alone in church, which was supposed to be her refuge from the gay world.

A victim of incest as a young child, Renae had never resolved her feelings of betrayal by a male figure in her family. God, she felt, had broken her trust also, since she blamed Him for the betrayal of her Christian roommate. It wasn't until she began dealing with feelings buried deep inside that she could accept God's unconditional love for her. Every time she failed, she felt God was mad at her and did not love her. Once she gained the assurance that God did not change His love based on her performance, she was able to spend more time reading the Bible and finding strength to resist temptations.

I showed her in Scripture that Satan is the one who comes to bring destruction to our lives. John 10:10 says, "The thief comes only to steal and kill and destroy; I [Jesus] have come that they may have life, and have it to the full."

Renae began to use the Scripture she was learning to countermand Satan's lies. When temptations came she would quote 1 Corinthians 10:13 and tell Satan that "this temptation is common to every man. God has given me the power to resist it, and I am not going to give in to the urges of my flesh just because you bring up some memory to tempt me." Several times a day she learned to resist Satan—and he did leave. Every day provided new opportunities for Renae to choose to do the right thing, although it was usually hard to feel good about the choice at the time.

A difficult lesson for all of us to learn is that doing right does *not* always feel good at the time, although it makes future choices easier; and the feeling good comes later, too.

People who struggle with feelings of homosexuality need to be assured that their identity is not to be established by those feelings, but by the Word of God. Encourage your friend to memorize and recite daily verses like 2 Corinthians 5:17, which we have already mentioned: "Therefore, if anyone is in Christ, he is a new creation; the old has gone, the new has come!" When the struggle comes with those deeply rooted feelings, the only sure foundation is Scripture.

An identity established in truth will never fluctuate with the instability of human emotion or desire. For, in fact, the battle for a soul takes place in the mind. The Christian's thought life is constantly under attack. Scripture provides ample exhortations to help us keep our thought lives protected from the evils of this world. Satan will remind us with subtle deception of experiences that have been pleasurable to us. This is an attempt to turn our thoughts from serving God. Foundational to psychology, after all, is the tenet that every action is preceded by a thought. Thoughts create emotions, which are eventually acted on.

Richard Mayhue, in his book *Unmasking Satan*, says, "Satan attempts to influence our minds so he can influence our lives. . . . Satan's chief activity in the lives of Christians is to cause them to think contrary to God's Word, and thus act disobediently to God's will."

Our need for a return to biblical principles is brought home daily as the newspapers report on the growing number of AIDS cases. Our generation must of necessity answer the call to holiness living. Only as Christian brothers and sisters, sons and daughters join the ranks is Satan truly unmasked. To help your friend break the hold of Satan on his life, suggest a prayer like the following:

"In the name of Jesus, I renounce my sexual involvement with ———. I renounce any involvements with witchcraft, horoscopes, the occult. [Be very specific here with anything the Lord brings to mind. If your friend has been involved with religious cults, have him renounce that involvement also.]

"Satan, I break your hold on my life now, and as an act of my will I submit to the Lordship of Jesus Christ and claim the blood of Jesus as my protection."

You can encourage your friend further by pointing out that temptation is not the same as sin. A major element in the healing of homosexuality is the realization that temptation is a common experience for us all. We are involved in sin only when we choose to act out a temptation.

Becky made contact with me after reading *Long Road to Love*. She was seeking healing from the guilt of numerous lesbian involvements over a five-year period. As I began to ask her questions, she told me it had been two years since she had acted out her feelings. She felt she was sinning when she even thought about homosexuality.

We went through Scriptures together and I showed her that guilt and condemnation come from the accuser of her soul, Satan, not from God. She had confessed her sin and vowed to turn from homosexual activity. The process of healing had simply not yet relieved her from the emotional remembrances of her past.

After several months of daily phone calls, Becky called one day in hysterical laughter. "I'm not guilty!" she roared. "I'm really not guilty!"

She finally understood that regardless of the temptation, if you do not give in, then God doesn't charge your thoughts against you in some sin tally in the sky. She had nothing to feel guilty about, which changed her entire concept of God and what it meant to live in relationship with Him.

Every person who has lived, including Jesus Christ, has been offered the opportunity to settle for a lesser standard than God's call to holiness. Every day we have the opportunity to yield to temptation in some form.

Self-gratification will always be part of the human condition and our carnal natures will be tempted to indulge in illicit pleasures, however subtle. To give in to indulgence is to feed an insatiable demon. Only the God who created us as sexual beings can empower us to behave with integrity and responsibility.

It might also encourage your friend or loved one to remember that healing is a process. An article in the August 18, 1989, issue of *Christianity Today* emphasized this process in the lives of leaders in the ex-gay movement. They gave the writer, Tim Stafford, an "overall . . . impression of health." He wrote:

> They were certainly not describing a quick 180-degree reversal of their sexual desires; rather, they described a gradual reversal in their spiritual understanding of themselves as men and women in relationship to God. They said this new understanding was helping them to relearn distorted patterns of thinking and relating. They presented themselves as people in process, though they were very clear that the process was well under way.

In this process, moreover, your friend is not alone. If he or she wants to change, then the God with whom nothing is impossible will show the way to victory.

When They Don't Want to Change

Giving encouragement and hope to someone struggling to overcome a problem can be a positive experience for most of us who want to help. But suppose the person you want to help scorns your good intentions and "suggests" you not try to change him. What then?

Many parents face this trauma as their children reject any discussion of their homosexual behavior, and sometimes cut off communication altogether. In these instances my advice is directed not to what you can help your loved one do, but to what *you* can do. This is an incredibly difficult situation because it appears to require so much passivity. Hang in there and follow these steps:

1. *Your attitude is vital.*

You are the only one you can change. You have to decide how to handle devastating information. You must choose either to keep an open line of communication or to refuse to discuss the situation. You must walk that fine line of accepting your loved one without accepting the sin.

2. *Take no direct action.*

If the person you are concerned about is an adult and living on his own, don't take any direct action. He is responsible to God for his own behavior. If you tried to intervene he would probably tell you to mind your own business, that he doesn't want to change. He would also probably resist printed material against homosexuality. Instead, keep those lines of communication open. He knows you don't approve. Your love in spite of what he knows you consider a bad decision will speak louder than words and begin to soften his heart toward the truth.

If he has a specific reason to feel angry toward you—for instance, rejection, divorce or parental abuse—seek his forgiveness. Helping him express his hurts is an important step toward healing.

3. *Be patient.*

When he does begin to talk about his situation, be sensitive while straightforward in relaying what the Bible says. Don't push too hard.

4. *Pray.*

This is the single most important thing you can do. You cannot change another person, but you can ask God to change his or her heart to desire health and wholeness. Ask the Lord for a mental picture of your loved one as a whole, happy and healed person and pray until it is a reality. Look for prayer support from others as well. It is crucial to find those with whom you can share. You will need a sense of Jesus' healing presence in your own life as you deal with disappointment, devastation, even possible guilt. If necessary don't hesitate to see a counselor.

Most people find it hard to believe that the best tool available in any life situation is prayer. It means, for example, that you cannot take over the reins of your child's life, but must leave that to God. If you relinquish your troubles to Him, He will act on your behalf.

Mrs. Morgan called a couple of years ago after reading my testimony in a local publication. She shared that her daughter Robin was a lesbian.

"She has some of your background," Mrs. Morgan said. "She went to a Christian college and it was there she became involved in homosexuality."

We talked for almost an hour about her daughter. Mrs. Morgan was determined to keep the doors of communication open—while believing God to work the miracle of healing for Robin. Before hanging up we prayed together. Mrs. Morgan said, "I'm keeping your number in my book. Right now Robin is in a relationship and doesn't want my help—but I know that someday she will and I want to be ready."

We hung up and over the months I forgot about her call. Then three months ago I found this message on my answering machine: "Darlene, this is Mrs. Morgan. I spoke with you last year. Robin is ready to find help. Will you meet with us?"

I did, of course, and Robin is now seeking a new life in a different town with different friends. She has only just begun her journey to wholeness, but Mrs. Morgan is one happy mother. God is continuing to answer her prayers.

Time alone will not bring healing to the homosexual; only prayer and the conviction of the Holy Spirit can draw that son or daughter—and other sons and daughters—into a place in which they grow disenchanted with the lifestyle and seek help. It won't be easy, but with enough patience—and these important basic first steps—you will eventually see changes taking place.

5

Finding the Way Out

To the family and friends of someone struggling with the sin of homosexuality or who has tested positive for AIDS because of homosexual activity, it is evident there are no easy answers.

The pathway to healing is not a smooth, flower-strewn walkway through peaceful gardens. It is a journey filled with jagged stones of choices and some irreversible consequences of past behavior. For the person with AIDS, it is a death sentence. For the person who has had multiple lovers and homosexual relationships, it is a path of painful memories. These former lovers are many times all too willing to entice the person who longs for healing back into a world of empty promises.

Those who make the choice to leave the homosexual world and develop a relationship with Jesus Christ must at the same time choose to be responsibile for past and future actions. In one sense, by deciding to live by biblical standards they enter the greatest struggle of their lives.

In the process of living an indulgent lifestyle, sin has been allowed to distort the mind, which now needs to be washed clean by the Word of God. Romans 12:2 says, "Do not conform any longer to the pattern of this world, but be transformed by the renewing of your mind. . . ."

It is in this time of resolution to change, to be transformed, that the family and Christian friends have the greatest opportunity to influence the lives of those who desire to overcome homosexuality. Along with teaching the first basic steps we discussed in the last chapter, Christian family members will need to support and encourage their loved one to develop new patterns of thinking, as well as find a support group of dedicated Christians.

The first four months after my own decision to leave the homosexual lifestyle, I experienced this type of accountability with other Christians when I became involved in a weekly Bible study and prayer group. I was given reading assignments and questions to answer in a spiritual progress notebook. I spent almost every nonworking hour reading my Bible or listening to Scripture tapes. Eventually I developed a sensitivity to destructive behavioral and thought patterns and asked God to change them. I wanted out of unhealthy relationships. Over a period of several months, with accountability to my prayer group, I was able to make positive choices that strengthened my commitment to walk in wholeness.

As part of this strengthening process it is often necessary to undergo what I call spiritual "surgery"—the removal of a long-time habit like masturbation or reading certain kinds of magazines or watching certain kinds of movies. Such habits are accompanied by destructive thought patterns that become firmly rooted strongholds of the enemy.

I learned to speak Scripture against those forces in my own life, and to use the authority of Jesus' name to break their influence over me. Slowly, but with a new confidence in God's ability to work in my life, I began the long process of healing.

Engaging in spiritual warfare and rebuking demonic forces did not solve my problem instantaneously. Although I knew Scripture and that Christ had indeed purchased full freedom for me on Calvary, I found that healing was more difficult to attain than simply by claiming the appropriate Scriptures.

It was more as if God lifted a veil from my eyes to show me that although I had the weapons of warfare, I was still the one who needed to battle in His strength. Until a specific experience of deliverance, I had been held captive by an intense yearning that had always pulled me back into homosexual relationships, no matter how much I tried to avoid them.

During the past several years of counseling others who struggle with homosexuality, I have discovered that I was not alone in this silent battle against a powerful force that pulls toward homosexual encounters. Without exception, those who attempt to come out of a homosexual lifestyle tell of an invisible magnet that tends to pull them toward others who are similarly magnetized. It is seemingly their "natural" reaction, an outgrowth of their sexuality.

Magnetic Attraction

Because of the obvious analogy, I was curious about magnets, and consulted the *World Book Encyclopedia* as to their nature and how demagnetization is possible.

Magnets are produced naturally , I learned, when pieces of lodestone attract other pieces of lodestone or other metallic iron fragments. Pieces of lodestone, if suspended by a thread, will orient themselves in a definite position with respect to the axis of the earth.

If a piece of soft iron is stroked with one of the polar ends of a lodestone, the metal will then exhibit the same properties of the lodestone. A magnet produced in this way or by an electric method is an artificial magnet. If the magnet is made of tempered steel or special alloys and magnetized by electric methods, it is called a permanent magnet because it retains those properties for a long time.

Surrounding any magnet is a field of force, which is strongest in the immediate vicinity of the magnet and progressively weaker at greater distances.

I discovered several correlations between the properties of a magnet and the "invisible magnet" that seems to dwell within persons wishing to find freedom from homosexual orientation. In the first place, we must have a spiritual foundation to orient ourselves, an anchor point of truth. Regardless of external circumstances, we need a place we can come home to and say, "This is truth!" This foundational axis is the Word of God.

To pull free from the force of homosexuality, we need special weapons. Second Corinthians 10:3–5 says,

> For though we live in the world, we do not wage war as the world does. The weapons we fight with are not the weapons of the world. On the contrary, they have divine power to demolish strongholds. We demolish arguments and every pretension that sets itself up

against the knowledge of God, and we take captive
every thought to make it obedient to Christ.

The pull toward sin, toward old habit patterns, is strong,
and there is seemingly no way to reprogram or demagnetize that force deep inside that wants to return to the
former way of living. First Corinthians 10:13, once again,
says that temptations are common to man . . . but that
God always has a plan. He has already made the way of
escape. Part of this "way" is described in Ephesians 6:10:
"Finally, be strong in the Lord and in his mighty power."
It is Christ's power at work in us that will demagnetize our
attraction toward sin.

The more we, like the magnet, associate with "like"-
magnetized persons—in this case, those committed to a
homosexual lifestyle—the stronger will be our own field of
magnetism. It is a matter of choice. If I had continued to
visit the same places where I found expression for my
homosexual yearnings, I would not have found the
strength to resist those homosexual urgings when they
began to surface.

For those persons for whom the gay environment has
been a life-support system, the magnetic hold is difficult to
break. This is possibly the most formidable battle the homosexual will face—that of separating himself from gay
friends and old habitats. Rationalizations and arguments
may sound so right when the person who struggles with
homosexual orientation explains why he cannot give up
those friendships. The deception: that the magnetic force
is too powerful to overcome.

Your responsibility as family or friend is to create a
supportive atmosphere for those attempting such a life

change. Family should be available not only to provide counsel, but to offer acceptance in the midst of the struggle. To extend friendship means to share in the everyday experiences of the one looking for freedom and wholeness. The need for acceptance is a deep human need, but especially for someone who has experienced a lifetime of rejection. As a new identity in Christ is established, we as the family of believers should not only teach the Bible with its guidelines for Christian behavior, but live it out in relationship with one another.

The more someone has been involved homosexually, the stronger will be the need he has created within himself, and the stronger his servanthood to sexual bondage. Paul exhorts us in Romans 6:16, "Don't you know that when you offer yourselves to someone to obey him as slaves, you are slaves to the one whom you obey—whether you are slaves to sin, which leads to death, or to obedience, which leads to righteousness?"

No Easy Answers

I have no simplistic solutions for change and realize that even if you take the homosexual struggler out of his environment, it does not take the homosexuality out of the person. Ceasing to do the acts of homosexuality does not make a person a heterosexual any more than doing heterosexual acts validates one's heterosexual orientation.

How we think about ourselves will be expressed in how we relate to others. Matthew 12:34 says, "For out of the overflow of the heart the mouth speaks." The heart is the very core of life, and what we fill our hearts with will oveflow to those around us. This is also why in Romans

12:2 we are told to "be transformed by the renewing of your mind." The mind here refers to the heart, the core of one's being. As our thinking is changed, our hearts are changed and our behavior is changed.

In reading about magnets, I discovered two ways to demagnetize a magnet, regardless of how it was produced.

One is by hitting the magnet with a hammer, thus causing a reduction in the magnetic force field. The atoms are scattered and the magnet is weakened, although it will still have a limited attraction field. (I don't recommend the use of a hammer to change the orientation of someone caught by homosexual attraction, however!) The only permanent way to demagnetize a magnet is to use extreme heat, which increases the motion of its atoms and permanently upsets their alignment.

Hebrews 12:29 says, "For our God is a consuming fire." Throughout Scripture there are references to fire burning out the dross or waste matter in our lives. In Jeremiah 23:29 we read, " 'Is not my word like fire,' declares the Lord, 'and like a hammer that breaks a rock in pieces?' " Again in Ephesians 5:26 we are told that God brings cleansing "to make her [all believers] holy, cleansing her by the washing with water through the word." It is the Word of God activated by the Spirit of God that brings cleansing and freedom.

Another verse, the now-familiar 1 Corinthians 6:11, is brought up-to-date as we recognize there is enough power in God's Word to demagnetize any attraction to homosexuality: "And that is what some of you were. But you were washed, you were sanctified, you were justified in the name of the Lord Jesus Christ and by the Spirit of our God." The Bible does not just *contain* the Word of God; the

Bible *is* the Word of God. And that Word is filled with unlimited power!

The process of walking into freedom is just that—a process. As family and friends, we need to allow that time to see healing working in their lives. While the initial release from the power of sin is instantaneous, the living out of that freedom happens day by day. What demagnetizes the desire for homosexual behavior is choices.

Frank Worthen in his book *Steps Out of Homosexuality* states there are three areas in the lives of people coming from a homosexual background that need correcting: their image of God, their image of others and their image of themselves. This is a radical transformation.

Frank explains how in our human nature we tend to blame anyone else for our condition, rather than assume responsibility for our own choices. When we do assume the responsibility, however, rather than play the "blame game," we can begin to grow in honest relationship with God and others.

The homosexual's perception of Christians must also change. Frank observes that often "homosexuals imagine rejection where none exists. Some assume that the heterosexual will not like the homosexual, so prejudice is assigned to him whether it's true or not." Most people involved in a homosexual or lesbian lifestyle have had their trust violated so many times that it takes time and commitment on the part of the family member or friend to develop rapport.

In addition to radical changes in their concepts of God, self and others, there are deep issues of self-worth that need to be addressed and healed. The tradeoff in the gay community for acceptance has been the prostitution of self-worth. Intimacy and sex have been seen as the best ways to relate to others, and *self* has been reduced to a commodity sold to the highest bidder. It is only as healthy Christian relationships of trust are developed that individual perceptions will change.

Frank Worthen writes that many people consult his ministry seeking acceptance and approval who are ambivalent about radical change. They want just enough to make their lives more comfortable, perhaps just enough bromide to take away the inner pain of isolation and rejection. If we are going to help our loved ones make the radical changes necessary to demagnetize the invisible magnet of homosexual attraction, however, we must help them deal with specific areas. To grow in freedom they must:

Accept Personal Responsibility

1. Acknowledge homosexuality as sin. If God says in His Word that something is sin, we can do no less.

2. Consider the Word of God as final authority for morality and behavior. Without such an anchor, they will drift on a sea of speculation and conflicting theories.

3. Acknowledge that Jesus Christ is the only answer for the healing of our sexual brokenness. I am convinced that there is no way out of homosexuality other than the power of Jesus Christ to transform orientation and behavior.

Avoid Blame

1. Assume responsibility for past choices and resolve to turn from this behavior forever. As much as is humanly possible, close doors to the past.

2. Refuse to look for someone or something to blame

71

for past choices. This doesn't mean to ignore environmental and psychological influences from the past that may have contributed to choices; it means starting over with God's help to overcome those influences.

3. Forgive anyone who has wronged them. Many lesbians and male homosexuals, as we have seen, were victims of incest or sexual child abuse. These events probably fractured their sense of self-worth and their ability to relate well to the opposite sex. These persons were victims, not responsible for the violent betrayals of trust inflicted upon them. Part of the healing process, however, involves forgiveness toward those who brought on this pain.

Often, it is helpful for them to find a victims' support group or private therapist with whom to work through these areas of victimization. Faith in Jesus Christ will not erase our past lives, but will allow us to grow beyond the events that have crippled our emotional and sexual responses.

Through our faith in Christ we begin to take control over our responses to those events in our lives. We allow the power of Christ to determine whom we become, rather than a series of events over which we had no control.

Find Christian Fellowship

1. Develop a regular study of the Bible with others and individually. Christian maturity requires more than church attendance. The best place for Christian growth and trust to happen is in small group prayer meetings and Bible studies.

2. Ask God to provide a mature Christian friend who will honor confidences and be available to pray with you in times of conflict. It is helpful if this can be a Christian couple, since this will provide interaction with same-sex and opposite-sex viewpoints.

Break with the Past

1. Break off contacts with people from a gay background, and refuse to participate in activities that involve that lifestyle.

Although this is the most direct action for healing, few people are able initially to abide by this recommendation. It is important to allow family and church family to help establish a new network of friends, which makes it easier to let the old drop away.

2. Learn to dress more appropriately in keeping with gender roles, and also change patterns of speech.

Many times women from lesbian backgrounds dress in a masculine fashion while some men have adopted feminine styles of clothing. It helps for them to have same-sex role models who can help develop appropriate dress.

One lesbian told me that for the first six months as a "straight" she felt hypocritical for wearing women's clothes. She felt as if she were "in drag" (dressing like the opposite sex) because she had lived so long in a masculine role.

One female impersonator who accepted Christ began to look and dress like a man for the first time in five years. Voices in his head screamed at him for months that he was a phony. He felt uncomfortable without the makeup and other trappings he had come to rely on for acceptance, but was determined to listen to God's voice of acceptance in the Scriptures. After a few months, with the caring of Christian brothers who spent time with him and encouraged him, the accusing voices of the enemy were silenced and he overcame his bondage to role reversal.

While breaking with the past is not always this dramatic, it does require a commitment to follow biblical guidelines. It is painful to leave the known. The role of family and friends in this transition time is to be available.

Wage Spiritual Warfare

While the external changes are a necessary part of healing for the person overcoming homosexuality, there is another area even more important to change. This is the thought life.

In this area the person must:

1. Use Scripture to break satanic oppression that comes against the mind and emotions. This is a primary requirement of spiritual warfare.

2. Renounce verbally the lifestyle and all sexual activities.

Satan will attempt to influence the thoughts by suggesting that change is impossible and even unnecessary in order to serve God. Sometimes well-meaning friends will aid in this deception by pointing out how many people have tried to go straight and failed.

The major weapon of offensive warfare is to open the Bible and read such verses as Luke 10:19–20: "I have given you authority to trample on snakes and scorpions and to overcome all the power of the enemy; nothing will harm you. However, do not rejoice that the spirits submit to you, but rejoice that your names are written in heaven."

Also, Philippians 2:9–10: "God . . . gave him the name that is above every name, that at the name of Jesus every knee should bow, in heaven and on earth and under the earth."

Scriptures that affirm the Lordship of Jesus and His authority over all evil powers should be memorized or read aloud during times of spiritual attack. Stand by your friend or loved one when such attacks come.

When I was first learning about spiritual warfare, I found it helpful to identify the nature of the attack. (What form was the oppression manifesting? Lust? Depression? Homosexual thoughts?) Then I would read Scriptures declaring that all things are subject to the name of Jesus. Finally I would address the "named" oppression like this:

> Lust [or depression or spirit of homosexuality], I take authority over you in the name of Jesus according to the Word of God. I resist you according to James 4:7, which says that if I submit to God and resist you, you must leave. I remind you, lust, that you have no power over me any longer, as I am a new creation in Christ Jesus, and I do not have to be a servant of sin any longer. I command you in the mighty name of Jesus and the authority of the Word of God, with the power of the blood of Calvary that is shed abroad in my heart, to leave me right now!

I found that satanic oppression could be resisted only in this manner. Sometimes I had to read the Scriptures for long periods before I felt release.

It was then that friends like Madeline from my Christian singles group were most influential. I could call anytime, day or night, if I needed prayer support. Madeline would pray right over the phone, and the additional strength in prayer was great encouragement.

God longs to show us that He does not hold our sins against us once we confess them and repent. We can only continue to know Him and see His heart revealed through the Scriptures.

We will not find a consistent message of hope any other place, for even the experiences of fellow believers have limitations. Our solid foundation is established in John 8:31–32: "If you hold to my teaching, you are really my disciples. Then you will know the truth, and the truth will set you free." Jesus continued a few verses later: "So if the Son sets you free, you will be free indeed" (verse 36).

Jesus is responsible for upholding His Word. We are responsible for committing ourselves to Him; then He can fulfill His promises in our lives. The message from the first-century Church still rings true in hearts today.

6

Helping Homosexuals Heal the Wounds of the Past

Imagine a Star Trek scene where someone is "beamed" to a distant planet and expected to relate to existing life forms.

For many homosexuals, the concept of wholeness is as foreign and scary as this imaginary trip into space. For these people, there has never been a framework of trust and intimacy that could foster healthy relationships. Often this lack traces back to childhood, to those situations of incest or other sexual molestation. Many times the event is repressed to such a degree that it is not in the conscious mind at all.

These hidden wounds of the past are often the strongest influence on choices to remain in same-sex relationships. They act as emotional fractures, but they can be healed.

It makes no difference whether we call it healing of memories, prayer healing, inner healing or healing for damaged emotions. In order to function as a whole adult, everyone must be able to integrate his childhood and his adult response to that childhood. This integration takes place deep inside as God Himself wraps up the hurt and, removing the pain, allows the individual to move forward in healthy relationships with others.

David Seamands suggests an appropriate image in his book *Healing for Damaged Emotions*: "You also need a deep inner healing of your memories to blot out the destructive, slow-motion video replays that interfere with the way you live."

Many homosexual responses seem to be triggered by an emotionally sensitive video replay that haunts a person with past experiences. He may have come into relationship with Christ and experienced forgiveness, but part of him is locked away from the freedom Christ has promised.

Liz told me she was distraught over her indulgence in fantasy, which always ended in masturbation. This, in turn, stirred up guilt. As she prayed for strength and read the Bible, she felt the Lord wanted her to deal with the root of the problem. Otherwise she did not feel she would be able to stop the constant replaying of a particular memory video.

After several sessions of our praying together, God revealed to Liz that the basis of her problem was low self-esteem. It was rooted in childhood experiences in which she was chosen last for team sports and was not popular like a younger sibling. She never felt special. Later, the role she assumed in lesbian behavior gave her a feeling of power. She was more assertive than her partners, which somehow filled her need not only to belong but also to be in control.

After her commitment to Christ, Liz felt insecure once again and part of a world that did not quite accept her. The fantasy life helped her feel special; it took away the loneliness for a time, and brought comfort to her fragile spirit. But the guilt that came in the morning always stole away any good feelings.

We decided to pray for a healing of her inner child, and ask Jesus to restore a sense of acceptance and specialness to Liz. We asked the Lord to bring back events of her childhood that had cut away at her self-image. During our prayer together, she thought of several incidents. We prayed and invited Jesus, with His healing touch, to be part of those scenes and to assure her of His acceptance.

Liz was released from her negative mental video and was able to understand why she had been locked into destructive behavior patterns. The Lord also revealed several root issues of attitude that had contributed to her involvement in homosexuality.

Understanding the root causes can help us as friends and family to be more understanding of adult behavior. It is through the eyes of the Spirit that we are able to look beyond the behavior of today and see the events that laid the foundation for it. Such revelations in prayer are never given as an excuse to condone sinful attitudes or actions, but as a key for healing memories, that wholeness might come.

In healing the wounds of the past it is important to keep in mind that our wounds were not inflicted in a day; likewise, healing does not come in an instant, snap-of-the-fingers prayer.

The causes of homosexuality are varied and unique with each individual. Only Jesus can go back to mend the brokenness. Required is a lifetime commitment to the process of living out one's Christianity. While an individual may be free from the compulsions of homosexual behavior, it may be years before he or she achieves emotional and spiritual maturity.

At a Pastoral Care conference in January 1990 in Southern California, Leanne Payne discussed some of the hindrances to this maturity. She has developed these concepts in her book *Crisis in Masculinity*. Specifically she states: "There are three major barriers to the maturity and wholeness of personality to which we are called. The first two—the failure to forgive others and the failure to receive forgiveness for ourselves—call for what we commonly refer to as the healing of memories. . . . The failure to accept ourselves is the third big block—and a healing and learning process is required that takes a little time."

I realized this process most significantly when I was sharing with Marie Hollowell recently some of my own struggles regarding self-discipline. I continue to look to her as my spiritual mentor when I am facing problems. It has always seemed that she, of all the Christians I know, has it all together, and I've appreciated drawing on her 75 years of wisdom.

This time she put her arm around me and chuckled in my ear. "My dear Darlene, I have news for you! God is doing more healing in my life now than ever before. This side of heaven, you'll never reach a place where there isn't need of His touch in many areas of your life."

I pulled back and looked her in the eyes. "What could God improve on in you, Marie?"

We both burst out laughing at my question. "Right!" I said. "I guess anyone who has arrived is already with

Jesus." I had drawn once again from a well of great wisdom.

Marie's honesty helps me realize that healing will continue to take place as long as we live. We make mistakes continually and are continually in need of healing from the effects of our choices.

Regardless of the circumstances that influence those choices, we must decide to change any destructive behavior patterns. If we have had a history of premarital sexual involvements, we need to ask God's forgiveness, repent of the sin and pray for healing in our soul. We must also ask for a breaking of any sinful emotional ties to our past.

Rita Bennett in her book *Making Peace with Your Inner Child* writes, "I've found that people's souls can be knit together for blessing or bondage. Someone who has had a premarital . . . or a homosexual love affair . . . may still be psychologically tied to the person with whom he had the affair. Such a tie must be broken."

She goes on to provide examples of prayers that can be used in a variety of circumstances to enter into complete cleansing and healing of memories. Many have found her book a valuable tool in the process of healing wounds of the past.

Healing of the memories is a spiritual renewing of the mind. With all the experiences of childhood, environment and negative choices as adults, it is evident that almost every person is a candidate for a mind renewing. Our goal: always to become more like Jesus.

Some have asked if a personal commitment to Jesus Christ is necessary in order to come out of a homosexual lifestyle. Given a proper understanding of wholeness—as healing for the total person—it is impossible to change without a personal relationship with Christ. I have heard of persons who have ceased their homosexual activity and are functioning in heterosexual relationships. While commendable, this is a behavior modification far short of the healing Christ has promised in the Scriptures.

In her book *Inner Healing through Healing of Memories* Betty Tapscott writes, "Every experience we have ever had is molded into our personality and makes us act the way we do. Psychologists tell us what happens to us in the first few years of life forms the basis for the way we act or react to situations for the rest of our lives."

If this is accurate, then it takes a power greater than psychology to transform our minds in such a way as to alter our behavior permanently.

No Pat Formula

We live in a world that encourages the instant. The food we eat, how we fix it and the information we require daily all declare our "instant" mindset. On television we can watch crimes committed, solved and prosecuted all within the scope of an hour.

It is not this way in the real world. In fact, nature teaches us repeatedly that things take time: The oak doesn't reach its full stature overnight; a foal ventures away from its mother only cautiously. For your friend or loved one committed to the process of inner healing, here are some basic steps.

1. *Find the roots.*

Encourage your friend to ask God to reveal any roots from childhood experiences that are affecting his adult life—emotional hurt, sexual or physical abuse, or sin that needs to be confessed.

God may point these out in a number of ways. He may speak to your friend's heart during prayer or give a word of knowledge during a prayer time with friends. He may speak through the Scriptures, causing a certain passage to "jump off the page." Or He may speak through a friend or counselor who can sometimes read emotional hurts more clearly than the individual involved. It is a good idea to ask the Lord to confirm any information your friend believes pertains to him.

Help your friend see that the important thing is to desire healing with his whole heart. Your job is to help prevent him from becoming discouraged in the process and to be supportive as he begins to realize the extent of the pains of the past.

2. *Pray for inner healing.*

Once your friend has asked Jesus to reveal root problems, wait with him in silence for the Holy Spirit to reveal an area on which to concentrate specific prayer.

This is the way I go about this portion of inner healing with those who come for prayer. I ask them to tell me what is coming to mind and let them share their thoughts. This in itself is sometimes a "confession" that opens the door to healing.

I may have received direction from the Holy Spirit already regarding an area for prayer, but I have learned to wait for the person to confirm it. This is a sign that he or she is ready to deal with that issue.

We then pray about the specific details. I ask Jesus to make Himself real to that "little person" who may have been victimized or who experienced rejection. I ask Jesus to bring comfort supernaturally to the little person who still lives inside the adult and who still feels the pain.

Often we will wait several minutes while he or she resolves any conflict in the spiritual realm. If there was childhood victimization, there are also deep anger and feelings of rejection that Jesus alone can heal.

In some cases one prayer session can yield dramatic results. But most often layer after layer of emotional pain is healed over several months. Such intensive prayer can be exhausting and there needs to be a space of time between prayer sessions. I encourage counseling friends to keep a record of their events of healing.

After each session we pray together and ask the Holy Spirit to come anew in a healing way and bring wholeness to the painful area.

3. *Ask for an infilling of God's Spirit.*

After a spiritual warfare session in which Satan's roots are identified and uprooted, it is important for the cleansing love of God to come in and fill those ravaged places. Romans 5:5 says, "And hope does not disappoint us, because God has poured out his love into our hearts by the Holy Spirit, whom he has given us." When healing becomes effective, the element of healing love will be administered by the Spirit Himself.

4. *Praise God for the healing.*

This is important not only because God deserves praise for His patient working in a person's life, but because it will thwart the devil's attacks of doubt and despair. When Satan's voice says, "You're trapped forever; you'll never change because there's no escape from all the bad things that happened to you," your friend can say, "Begone, Satan! I choose to praise God because He is good. He is faithful and kind and pours out His healing love into my heart."

5. *Learn to forgive.*

Perhaps the most important step in the process of healing the wounds of the past is learning to forgive and be forgiven. Both are equally difficult in the first steps of the journey. Forgiveness is a decision, a choice of will that may or may not have good feelings attached. People who have lived a homosexual lifestyle generally have innumerable persons they must forgive, and others that they must ask to forgive *them*.

Have your friend ask the Lord to bring each of these persons to mind. Then pray about whether to contact them in person or in writing. (He may feel he should.) If he needs to ask forgiveness of family and friends hurt by his decision to live as a homosexual, encourage him to seek reconciliation.

Since more than eighty percent of the lesbians I have counseled or known have been victims of sexual abuse, this is a major area for forgiveness.

Any woman who seeks healing from lesbianism and who has been a victim of sexual abuse needs to work toward forgiving the perpetrator. She likely has a deep reservoir of anger and hostility that will only feed a multitude of destructive emotions until forgiveness becomes a reality.

Jan Frank in her book *A Door of Hope* suggests four stages of forgiveness for the victims of incest: "First, I must acknowledge or own up to the pain. Second, I must release my right to hold onto the bitterness, resentment and anger. Third, I must desire reconciliation. Fourth, I must extend to the offender an invitation to rebuild the relationship through the expression of unconditional love and acceptance."

The biblical principle of forgiveness will work a transformation in the life of the person committed to forgiving. It may not always result in reconciliation with the one being forgiven, but it will remove any barriers between you and God in your own healing.

Babs found the lack of reconciliation to be a painful fact in her life. She had struggled with same-sex attractions for as long as she could remember. After several telephone conversations, I brought up the issue of incest. I told her it was frequently a contributing factor in the lives of women who struggle with lesbianism.

Babs assured me she had never been molested. She felt she had been born with homosexual feelings. But she agreed to pray with me that God would reveal to her the source of this female attraction.

Within weeks, Babs called in a panic because of a newly recurring nightmare. In it she could see her father molesting her as a very young child. Her conscious mind rejected the pictures, but they disturbed her greatly.

I recommended a professional Christian therapist who could guide her in ways that I was not qualified to do. After several months of therapy, Babs not only acknowledged the molestations, but felt she was prepared to confront her father.

We discussed at length the possible outcome: either forgiveness and reconciliation, or denial. She felt she was prepared for either.

Because her parents were Christians, Babs anticipated repentance and the healing of the strained relationship she had with her father. That never happened.

Both parents denied that any situation such as she described could ever have occurred. Her brothers and sisters turned against her for stirring up trouble. Babs' longing for support and acceptance faded.

It has been almost two years and Babs struggles daily with loneliness. She is learning not to take on blame for the molestation or the family rejection. Still in professional therapy, she is learning how not to remain a victim. She has chosen to forgive her father—and the rest of her family—because that is what the Bible teaches, and because Babs wants nothing to hinder her own healing from the attraction to homosexuality.

The process of healing is a painful one, but without the process, there is no hope of healing at all.

6. *Receive forgiveness.*

Along with forgiving others and asking their forgiveness comes the added benefit of being able to receive God's forgiveness. We all need a deeper understanding of the reality that Jesus Christ is for us, and not against us.

As we bring our sinfulness to Him and confess it, we receive complete forgiveness. We no longer need to feel guilty about the past. We no longer need to feel shame over sexual brokenness or any past behavior. In that moment, we receive the fullness of God's forgiveness and acceptance.

The wounds of the past will leave scars, but the painful sting of regret will be healed. The scars will remind us of where we have been without Jesus and, more importantly, where we are with Him as our Savior.

Scars are strong reminders of healing. They are also reminders of hope for those who have yet to begin the process of healing the hurts of the past. Scars can be reminders of God's grace, both to the homosexual and to the family that loves him.

7. *Maintain a journal.*

It is a good place to record prayers, goals and conversations with the Lord. Also, it provides encouragement when Satan tempts your friend to think nothing has changed. He can record new ideas or insights that he receives from Scripture, and determine to incorporate them into his life.

8. *Ask God for a network of accountable prayer partners.*

I stress *network* because it is easy to fall into a dependent or exclusive relationship if your friend has only one person who knows him well. There should be several people in his life with whom he can talk freely regarding the struggles he experiences in the inner healing process. These will not all be struggles of a homosexual nature, but will encompass every area of Christian growth.

A specific accountability relationship is beneficial particularly for times of sexual temptation. Needed is a mature Christian of the same sex who is willing to be available as a prayer partner at any time.

In the past there has been accountability abuse by groups that wanted to dictate behavior to their members. We have individual responsibility for our choices that can never be overridden. In James 5:16, on the other hand, we read, "Therefore confess your sins to each other and pray for each other so that you may be healed." I believe we are accountable to make our needs known to other Christians so they can pray with us and facilitate our healing.

"Self-examination can only take me so far," writes James M. Houston in an article entitled "The Independence

Myth" (*Christianity Today*, January 15, 1990). "I need others to help expose and help me understand where sin would deceive and confuse me."

Then, as we learn to assume full responsibility for our actions, God is able to complete our healing. As long as I blame someone or something for my condition, I will actually prevent this from happening.

9. *Submit to Christ's Lordship.*

Often there are relationships, involvements or possessions we might like to retain as "harmless" reminders of our past. Yet even nonsexual relationships can contain elements that hinder the inner healing process.

Perhaps the Lord will reveal specific things that should be tossed away: pictures, books, jewelry, etc. These can represent emotional ties to the past. If your friend becomes convinced God is asking him to part with such items, he should be obedient and destroy them. *Any* occult items should be burned. Clothing items that are a reminder of a homosexual lifestyle should also be destroyed.

Above all, however, let the Lord be in charge.

Jessie called me after reading *Long Road to Love*. She felt that if I could change after so many years, God could bring healing to her life, too. We spent several hours sharing about Christ and my healing process. I prayed with her for a total commitment of her life to Christ, and that He would guide her on a path of wholeness.

Over the next few weeks Jessie cleaned house spiritually. She began to throw away clothing, pictures and items given her by former lovers. She tried to switch from cowboy boots and Western shirts to feminine clothing that would be more acceptable in church.

I encouraged her to spend a little more time building an inner biblical foundation rather than try mainly to "look good" on the outside. She wanted instant success, however. She also felt she could resolve her conflicts better if no one at her new church knew she had been gay.

Within three months Jessie was discouraged and angry with the church, with her faith that didn't "fix" everything and with me. She said I had made her "give up" everything. Though I pointed out that it had been her choice to clean house, she held me responsible personally for her unhappiness.

I didn't hear from her for almost a year, although I continued to drop her notes and pray for her. When she did contact me again, she had quite a different attitude.

"God never let me alone no matter what I did," she confessed. "And He kept telling me He was more interested in how I responded to Him in my heart than how I looked to the world!"

Change came slowly, but it did come, along with a new submissiveness to serve God.

For those within the Body of Christ as well as family members who struggle with homosexuality, encouragement is needed. The externals will change in conjunction with the transformation of the inner person.

10. *Develop healthy relationships.*

A large part of inner healing for the person who struggles with homosexuality is discovering that he or she can have same-sex friendships and not be tempted sexually. The person who has lived in the gay lifestyle for a while has to learn how to develop these healthy friendships.

Sometimes, for instance, the person who struggles with same-sex attraction is tempted to put meanings into the actions of others that were not intended. Not every hug means sexual attraction.

If feelings of attraction begin to influence behavior toward a brother or sister in Christ, they should be confessed as sin. The person to whom your friend is accountable in this area should pray with him about this. Under no circumstances should he go to the individual and confess the attraction. Such a confession would either alienate the other person or attract him in an unhealthy way.

Let me close this chapter by emphasizing the fact that the attainment of inner wholeness takes time. There will probably be slips and mistakes along the way, and when this happens Satan is quick to tell your friend that he or she has not changed at all. Remember, Satan is a liar. If he starts in with accusations, your friend is probably on the right road to healing. Onward with the process!

7

Specific Help for Families and Friends

As complex as the problem of homosexuality is, it is equaled by the pain of family members.

Parents, siblings and friends all seek to relate in a healing way to the one who struggles with homosexuality. While no one set of guidelines covers every situation, the suggestions in this chapter can plant some seeds of hope and provide some answers.

I was nineteen when I first told my mother of my lesbian involvement. I was attending a Christian college, preparing for the mission field. Then I became involved in a lesbian relationship with a friend who also attended the college.

I left school, confused about my calling and my sexual orientation. All my mother knew was that I had moved to California to spend some time with my father.

Mom did not know I was spending most of my time in

a gay bar. That is, until I got drunk one night and decided to call her and tell her I was a lesbian. I felt sure she and Dad were mostly to blame for my homosexual feelings. I had never vented my anger and hurt over their divorce or my shattered childhood.

The night I called I let the entire volcano of hurt and pain erupt. I was yelling when I ended my call with, "So now you know! I'm a lesbian. I'll never have children to hurt like you hurt me."

When I hung up the phone, I was racked by convulsive sobs. *Now I'm free*, I thought. *I've finally come out to my family and I don't need to hide anymore.*

It wasn't until years later, long after I had restored my relationship with God, that I learned my mother's reaction.

Mom told me she was shocked and devastated. She did not know what to do or where to go for help in understanding me. She tried to find some books but could find nothing. Finally she made an appointment with her medical doctor, just to get some advice. She didn't know he was a Christian, but she felt he could provide some direction.

The doctor shared what he knew about homosexuality from a medical standpoint, then advised her just to love me. Only God, he told her, could change me. But my mother was not a Christian at this point, and our relationship became so strained that we did not speak for almost a year.

Once we started talking again, we had no common ground to discuss my choice of a lesbian lifestyle, so our conversations carefully excluded any mention of homosexuality. I interpreted her silence on this subject as consent.

Almost two decades later, as Mom was reading the proofs for my book *Long Road to Love,* she shared her pain. God began a restoration of our relationship that continued until her death in 1988.

Many parents confronted with the news of their children's homosexuality are, unlike my mother, Christians. These parents' emotional responses are equally devastated, but with this added pain: "How could this happen in a *Christian* family?"

In the book *How Will I Tell My Mother?* Jerry Arterburn shares his story. He was raised in a Christian family, attended an evangelical church, taught Sunday school, went to a Christian college . . . and ended up in an AIDS ward. His lifelong secret could no longer be withheld from his parents.

In his mother's words: "The news that Jerry was homosexual was a total shock. I was filled with fear and disbelief. I was anguished to learn that he had the deadly virus AIDS."

She expresses the heartbreak of mothers around the world. But many parents and family members abandon the AIDS patient and refuse to be reconciled. Clara Arterburn and her husband, Walter, are among the minority of parents who have chosen to love their sons who have been diagnosed with AIDS. They have prayed for grace to go through this difficult and painful experience of watching their child die of complications from the virus.

Jerry's mother gathered him in her arms and loved him, assuring him she would be there to help no matter what. Her response helped Jerry repent, reaffirm his faith in Christ and know that when he did die he would go to be with the Lord. Although God forgave his sin, Jerry, like all of us, received the consequences of sin.

But what if you do not feel that loving and accepting just yet? What if your son or daughter has just announced that he or she is gay and you have not recovered from the shock? What if AIDS has been someone else's problem, and you don't even want to think of its touching your life?

Support Groups

In your initial pain you may feel alone, as if no one else in the world could possibly understand what you are going through. It is helpful to know that others do, and that there are support groups all around the country. Others have learned to survive this emotional devastation. You can, too.

One such group is Spatula Ministries in La Habra, California. Barbara Johnson founded the group more than ten years ago when her son taught her firsthand that Christian families are not immune to the pain of a child's choosing a homosexual lifestyle. Barbara's initial reactions are recorded in her book *Where Does a Mother Go to Resign?* She says she decided to call the ministry Spatula because you need a spatula to peel yourself off the ceiling when you first find out your child is gay.

She looked for help from ministers, T.V. evangelists, doctors and anyone she could find who knew anything about homosexuality. What evolved was the formation of her group, because what she found more than answers were hundreds of parents also looking for answers. This group now ministers to parents around the world. (See Appendix II for address.)

Intervention Steps without a Parents' Group

Until you find a group, there are some things you can do for yourself. Some we have already touched on in chapter 4.

1. *Try not to panic.*

This is easier to hear than to pull off when your child has just informed you of a homosexual preference. Some parents find out by accident, which can intensify the feelings of anger and betrayal.

Remember that nothing has changed suddenly about your child. He or she has simply chosen to reveal to you what has been part of his or her life for some time. It will not help to try to use logic or Christian teaching at this point. Homosexuality is an emotional response, not a logical decision.

2. *Try to maintain open communication in the relationship.*

This is your son or daughter; nothing can ever change that fact. If you attack his choice or condemn her as sinful and going to hell, you will break off any opportunity to help.

Remember: It is the *behavior* of homosexuality that is sin. Your child may be confused about that fact and have decided he is irrevocably homosexual because of same-sex attraction. He may or may not have already acted upon such feelings. Try to find out how committed he is to this behavior and lifestyle and what has caused him to identify himself as homosexual.

Across the country there are teenage groups even in junior high that think it is "cool" to be homosexual or bisexual. Many of these kids have no idea what this actually means. They are looking for identification and acceptance from their peers, as well as a reaction from society.

3. *Secure information on homosexuality and AIDS.*

If you are not informed on factors that may contribute to a homosexual choice, go to the library or your Christian bookstore or write Exodus for material. You should also be aware of what the Bible says about homosexuality, especially 1 Corinthians 6:9–11.

> Do you not know that the wicked will not inherit the kingdom of God? Do not be deceived: Neither the sexually immoral nor idolators nor adulterers nor male prostitutes nor homosexual offenders nor thieves nor the greedy nor drunkards nor slanderers nor swindlers will inherit the kingdom of God. And that is what some of you were. But you were washed, you were sanctified, you were justified in the name of the Lord Jesus Christ and by the Spirit of our God.

What hope! According to St. Paul there were Corinthian Christians who used to be gay, but now had been changed and were serving the Lord Jesus. Today there are people in every denomination across the land who were formerly bound by homosexual sin and are now washed, set apart for God's use and fully restored by His power. I know because I am one of them. Daily lives are being changed by the power of Christ, which is greater than any sin, including that of homosexuality. Don't lose hope for your son or daughter.

4. *Find a prayer partner.*

This is the most important thing you can do for yourself. If you have at least one other person with whom you can share, you will move more quickly into healing. Make opportunities to pray and share your emotional struggle. We often need another person to give us perspective on an emotionally explosive situation, and this prayer partner will provide that perspective.

The feelings you experience may be very much like the grief experienced at the death of a loved one. There will be shock, anger, denial and eventually acceptance. The acceptance is not of the sinful behavior, but of the person you love.

5. *Find release for any guilt feelings you may have.*

Remember, you are not to blame for the choices of your children. You may have been the best parent you could be with the information and resources you had. Your children are responsible individually for how they live out the choices of their lives.

If you feel, on the other hand, that you have failed in your responsibility, go to God and ask forgiveness. Do not carry the guilt of imperfection. No parent has ever reared a child without making mistakes along the way, and no parent ever will.

Strengthening your relationship with the Lord will provide the foundation for your child to evaluate his relationship with you and with God.

It is also important to realize that even if you do all the "right" things from here on in, your child may never choose to leave the homosexual lifestyle. He or she may choose to continue in this sin, just as people choose to continue in any sin. You can pray for him, ask God to intervene in his life, ask God to protect him from harm and deadly diseases. But ultimately the decision as to whether he will seek change is up to him.

I have found that it sometimes takes many years for a person to decide gay is not happy and to start looking for alternative resources.

Your love and acceptance of your child should be demonstrated clearly, and just as clear should be your underlying conviction that homosexual actions are sin that can be cleansed.

Arguments from Pro-Gay Churches

You may hear a variety of pro-gay arguments, especially if your child is involved in a religious group such as the Metropolitan Community Church, that homosexual relationships are a gift from God and that a person is born that way and cannot change his orientation.

Scriptures advocating loving acceptance and nonjudgmental attitudes will be quoted out of context. Any comments you might make on the behavior of homosexuality will be construed as personal condemnation. These are situations you can be prepared to address by knowing exactly what the Bible does say about sexual responsibility for every individual.

It is also good to be prepared with information on Christian groups staffed by ex-gays to substantiate that change is possible. On the other hand, I have spoken with leaders of ex-gay ministries around the world who have come under attack from pro-gay activists. Their testimonies are dismissed with a number of explanations.

Sometimes they say the person was never really gay, just confused in his thinking.

This argument is a bit naïve when you consider that

some who have been redeemed from the lifestyle were involved heavily for more than fifty years.

Sometimes the activists state that if we were gay, then we still are, but are repressing our sexuality. This is a hard argument to counter except by personal testimony like that of the blind man healed by Jesus: "One thing I do know. I was blind but now I see!" (John 9:25).

Some groups have even attempted to set up leaders in order to discredit their testimonies. They have had a gay person come for "counseling" and try to engage the leader in a sexual encounter. Although the tactics vary, the pro-gay groups want to use any means available to substantiate "once gay, always gay." One ministry leader told me that even after he was married, a gay newspaper reported it had "positive proof" he was living secretly with a male lover.

Pro-Gay Goals for the Future

As the parent or friend of someone who has chosen the homosexual lifestyle, you should be aware that he or she may be identifying not just with sexual behavior but with an entire subculture. There is a political movement that has vowed to put new meaning into the term *gay nineties*. Depending upon your friend's or child's commitment to the cause, he or she could become very hostile if you oppose its goals. Christian beliefs and traditional family values will be ridiculed, as pro-gay elements in society press for homosexual marriages and full status as a recognized minority.

Not all who embrace the lifestyle become political activists, but the numbers of those who demonstrate openly for these and other gay rights are growing.

In the face of such open support is a growing trend of passive resistance across our nation. Almost everyone has a friend or acquaintance who is gay, and when no Christian standard is held up against homosexual behavior, the philosophy becomes "live and let live." Some may wonder if it is worth it to take a stand against this lifestyle at the risk of losing a friend or family member. They are confused by reports that as much as ten percent of the population may be gay. If so many are coming out and stating they were born gay, how can such numbers be refuted? Is it possible they are right?

For Christians, this question must be settled with one immovable foundational truth: the Bible. Unless the standard of the Scriptures is established, all discussions will end in angry disagreement.

Homophobia

What does this term mean that is used as an accusation against the straight community? Basically, it means to be afraid of homosexuality. The truth is, however, the gay community uses it to attack anyone who does not accept the homosexual lifestyle.

God's truth is that homosexuality is sin, and sin separates anyone from fellowship with Him. When people oppose this behavior based on the clear witness of the Bible, they are not homophobic; they are rightly dividing the Word of truth. It is a biblical declaration, not a homophobic reaction.

If someone chooses to persist in sinful activity, the consequence of that sin can be both physical and spiritual death. This, too, is a biblical principle, not a homophobic declaration.

At the same time, some Christians conceal fear or even hatred of homosexuals behind an ostensibly biblical front. Charges of homophobia in these cases are right on target. We need to be careful, then, that we guard the attitudes of our heart and distinguish carefully between the sin and the sinner.

God's Purpose in Defining Sin

To help you keep a clean perspective as you try to help someone out of a homosexual lifestyle, remember that from the viewpoint of God the Father, one sin is not more terrible than another. Any sin—observe the "impartial" lists in 1 Corinthians 6:9–10, 2 Timothy 3:2–5 and Galatians 5:17–21—separates a person from God.

This understanding is important when dealing with those in a homosexual struggle. They need acceptance, love and the affirmation of their uniqueness as God's creations. The behavior of acting out homosexually, however, must be identified as sin, just as we identify adultery or gossip as sin.

I have come to understand better in recent years the nature of sin. The reason God places limits on our behavior is so that we will not be separated from His fellowship. Some may think He limits us because He doesn't want us to enjoy life, but that is not true. He wants us to participate fully in activities that will give us a sense of well-being and rightness with Him.

When we sin, we immediately feel bad, or at the very least strained in our fellowship with Him. We then tend to avoid spending time with Him. The reason God hates sin is that it separates us from what He desires most for us, intimate fellowship with Him.

A recent acquaintance, Barbara, exemplifies this separation. She was reared in a Christian home and attended a Southern Baptist college. While there she started drinking, and for more than twenty years now she tells me she has been in and out of treatment programs. She feels she can't give up alcohol and she does not want to give up her relationship with Christ. He has never let her be satisfied with the life she is living, and she has never found a "cure" that takes away her craving for alcohol. She has, at times, gone several years without a drink, but something always brings her back.

Barbara had studied to become a missionary and still feels God's call on her life. Yet when she phones, I can tell she has been drinking. I ask her, "Barbara, have you gone back to church? Are you getting the support you need to overcome your problem?"

"No," she replies. "This is a small community. I can't let anyone know I am back on the booze."

"Then have you gone to God and asked forgiveness so He can help you overcome the problem?"

"No." Her deep Southern accent is slurred with alcohol. "God can't help me till I quit drinking. You're the only one I can talk to about this because you don't really know me."

The very thing she needs, she feels unwilling or unworthy to receive. Although we have prayed together and Barbara wants to "be right with God," she feels God will not accept her in her current condition.

Barbara is on an endless treadmill of depression and alienation from God. She needs to grasp the truth that

God is for her, not against her. He wants to bring healing into her life. She, like all of us, must come to Him as she is, knowing she is unable to change herself. This is, after all, the most basic manifestation of grace—God's ability to enable us to do what we cannot do in our own ability. We received salvation through grace, and our ability to move along in healing is a continuing work of that grace.

How Will They Hear? How Will They See?

Sometimes I get frustrated when I talk with people like Barbara who need much more than someone to tell them there is hope to change their sexual orientation. They need a spiritually mature friend who will walk them through the Scriptures and show them what a relationship with Jesus will do in their lives. Often we stop our teaching with the gift of salvation. We fail to communicate the reality of Jesus' involvement in every area of life.

My friend Ed, who writes from Texas, struggles with this reality. He is a male prostitute in his early twenties. He accepted Christ as his Savior about three years ago. He goes to church on Sunday, takes evening classes several days a week and finances his existence by paid homosexual encounters.

As we have discussed biblical standards for sexual responsibility, Ed admits he knows Jesus does not approve of his actions. But he asks, "How can I get an education and make something of myself unless I have a place to stay and money coming in to pay the rent?" He does not want to prostitute for the rest of his life and he expresses concern about AIDS, but he sees no way out.

I know God has a better plan for Ed, but I don't know

how to convince him of God's sufficiency to meet his practical needs. I pray for a Christian family who will "adopt" Ed, but so far Ed still turns tricks to survive.

Bret from Oregon is another young man learning to find God's sufficiency in ways that affirm his manhood. Bret is also in his early twenties. Although he has never acted on them, homosexual fantasies used to be as much of his daily routine as eating breakfast. Bret never related well to his father and looked for fulfillment through the acceptance of other males. He was attracted to men who appeared strong and decisive. He compared himself in a negative way because he was not married and did not have a job and a life goal of successive achievements like other men his age.

Together, we reaffirmed Bret's relationship to Jesus. We discussed ways of interaction with Christian male role models who would build him up, rather than make him feel inferior. And we found Scriptures that affirmed his acceptance by Christ, who was wholly male in gender and orientation.

Bret is beginning to feel good about himself, and has gradually been able to replace his sexual fantasies with a confession of the reality of God's heterosexual intent for him. Bret knows now that this is true regardless of his marital or job status.

The process of Bret's healing has included professional therapy, ministry by mail and phone, and a dedicated effort on his part to search the Scriptures for ways he can control negative thoughts. He now realizes he is not a homosexual just because of an attraction to male role models. Sexual attraction revealed a deeper need for intimacy and for a change in his own self-esteem. Bret believes God has healthy relationships available so he will learn how to be a godly Christian man and in full control of lustful desires. With growing understanding of himself, the Scriptures and basic human nature, he is becoming more self-assured. God is teaching him about his maleness, and is working giant steps of maturity into his life. Plus, Bret has developed a healthy relationship with a deacon in his church who is teaching him about friendship.

"I don't want to be gay," Bret said to me recently. "Now I see that I don't have to be gay. God really does have something better for me."

This realization did not come overnight for Bret, nor does it for hundreds of people I talk to. I have seen first-hand that before any significant changes are made in homosexuals' lives, there must be at least three elements present or they will not be able to hear with their hearts the message of hope. These elements, which you can help provide, are genuine friendship, acceptance and trust.

Friendship

Many well-meaning Christians want to protest and "out-legislate" pro-gay bills in the state senate. Not as many want to cultivate a friendship that will help change the heart of a person struggling with homosexuality. The behavior of every person alive will change only as his or her heart is changed. While changing hearts is God's responsibility, offering genuine friendship is ours.

Friendship includes honesty when confronting a person about his behavior if it is inconsistent with biblical teaching. The purpose of confrontation, however, should always be reconciliation to Christ, not just to make "me" as a straight more comfortable

There are endless debates on befriending a practicing homosexual. The question is how to accept the person without accepting the sin. I think when we make our position clear regarding the sin of homosexuality, we can offer Christian friendship and not appear to accept the behavior. If a person never finds this type of acceptance in another, he or she may never experience Christ's acceptance and forgiveness.

Acceptance

Until people come to understand God's acceptance, they cannot respond to His love. People recognize when they are being manipulated just to become a "conversion" statistic. They can sense if they are being accepted, and if you really care about them.

When you share from your heart that you want God's best for them, they will listen—if you have offered them acceptance. This is true "friendship evangelism."

It is often helpful to share how Christ has met your own needs, and to offer to pray that He will meet theirs. This is especially effective for those people who have some Christian training. Love takes time to work its changes, but it is more effective than condemnation.

Trust

Almost without exception, Christians who struggle with homosexuality will be hesitant at first to share their stories. They fear not only rejection, but betrayal and exposure in their church communities. To be a friend means we must be trusted to keep their confidence. If we betray that trust, we will lose a friendship and the opportunity to help in the healing process.

Now for a word of warning: Believe it or not, sometimes in trying to help a friend we can fall ourselves.

An Unexpected Trap

The past few years have brought an alarming increase in the number of calls and correspondence I have received from married women who have fallen into lesbian relationships within the church. Although each situation is different, one of the partners usually has previous sexual experiences in her background, often from childhood. Many times the feelings from those events have never been acknowledged, let alone resolved. Suddenly the feelings have erupted in a strongly dependent relationship with a Christian friend, often in the helper role. Then the friend has become involved herself by trying to help.

Recently I was counseling two women who are leaders in their church denomination. They had been friends for a long time. They knew the Bible regarding homosexuality and regarding temptation and how to resist it. Yet they now found themselves involved in a lesbian relationship.

"Neither of us wanted this to happen," Sara whispered. The heavy weight of guilt was evident in her voice and in the look of despair in her eyes. "It was a Christian friendship. We were really close and everything just exploded."

I looked at her friend Peggy. "What about you?" I asked. "What do you think caused this friendship to move from godly to sinful?"

Peggy's brown eyes brimmed with tears. "I don't know.

I love Sara. She's everything I always wanted to be. Something just happened. . . ."

On the surface, I could agree that something had indeed happened, and now their lives were twisted into a distortion that neither had wanted. But now neither wanted to be totally released, either.

Ronald and Joanne Highley make an interesting point here: "This condition being un-asked for is why many homosexuals will say as adults that they were 'born that way' and should be given the freedom to pursue their 'sexual preference.' However, men can love men without sexual desire for each other, and so can women."

The problem occurs when emotional dependencies and individual deficits attract people to one another. Their relationships, however significant, cannot be healthy ones until these issues are resolved.

Relationships like that between Sara and Peggy are described and examined in a booklet by Lori Thorkelson, *Emotional Dependency: A Threat to Close Friendships*. Thorkelson shows that long before physical involvement, there is an emotional setup of dependency.

If you recognize a problem developing, she suggests these steps:

1. Make a commitment to honesty.

2. Change activities that would lend themselves to too much intimacy.

3. Allow God to work. Spend time in prayer and Bible study on your own.

4. Prepare for grief and depression.

5. Cultivate other friendships.

6. Resolve the deeper issues (e.g., sexual abuse).

7. Prepare for the long haul. It's a process.

Each step is presented as part of an ongoing decision-making process, difficult at times, yet rewarded in the eventual formation of healthy relationships.

If each person is committed to being the person God has called her to be, and to developing a relationship with Jesus at the center, then the chain of emotional dependency can be broken. Sometimes this will involve a complete break with the person, but not always.

A premise for the type of counsel applied to individual situations is presented by Elizabeth Moberly in her book *Homosexuality: A New Christian Ethic.* She presents the homosexual condition as being a same-sex deficit in the early years of development.

In the past, treatment of gay men and lesbians has been based on separating them from the lifestyle or from their immediate relationships, with the hope that isolation will bring healing. Moberly suggests that trying to prevent same-sex contact will in fact *prolong* the healing process, because healthy same-sex relating is the very thing needed. What psychology and the Church have long viewed to be the problem may in fact be part of the "cure."

Sometimes the situation is complicated when the entangled persons attend the same church or have the same employer. But it is possible to see each other every day and not allow physical involvement.

Until the emotional dependency is broken, maintaining a healthy friendship is impossible. The reprogramming of the "hooks" that locked in the dependency must be identified and healed. I believe that both persons involved must be committed Christians and have separate support systems in order for this to occur. The tendency to fall into sin will be strong, so both persons must rely on God's unlimited healing ability.

Jennifer found the principle of separation to be effective. She had become a Christian recently, and the Lord was dealing with her to break off a wrong relationship with her roommate. Jennifer was willing to give up the sexual involvement, but adamant that the friendship not be terminated. At Jennifer's insistence her roommate moved out. They talked by telephone daily, and still attended many social functions together.

Because Jennifer had changed her behavior, she no longer felt she was sinning, yet she still struggled with homosexual yearnings. The conflict had her on the verge of an emotional breakdown.

I agreed with Jennifer that it is the *behavior* of homosexuality that the Bible condemns, yet the same Bible promises freedom and wholeness, not a frustrated, tormented existence.

After we prayed, Jennifer agreed to cut off social events with her friend for two weeks. During this time she agreed to spend time with new friends at church and more time reading her Bible. She began to find new strength to overcome the emotional bonding with her former roommate. The two weeks were extended and soon Jennifer was surprised at how she had transferred her dependency to the Lord instead of another person.

If healing is going to come to anyone who struggles with difficult areas of sin in his or her life, it will come with a return to basics—a return to that first-love experience with Jesus.

Jennifer still cares for her former roommate, but they have nothing in common since the roommate is not interested in a relationship with Jesus. I asked Jennifer what had happened in her life since she decided to put Christ first.

Her eyes sparkled. "I keep falling in love with Jesus. I knew Him as my Savior . . . but now I love Him more. He's my very best friend."

Our Main Message

It may sound too simple, but I am convinced that if we are going to reach our friends and loved ones, our main message must be this: Christ came into the world to save sinners. He came to make sick people well and broken people whole. We cannot be healed emotionally until our spirits are energized by the Spirit of God in the experience of the new birth. The process of healing cannot even begin until the miracle of redemption has taken place. Then it may take years of spiritual restoration for us to approach wholeness.

Because the promise of Jesus is to make us well in every respect, the result of His relationship with us is healing. We will find acceptance in Him, and learn to trust that all the changes He wants to work in our lives are for good.

As a friend or family member who cares, you have a challenge to plant seeds of truth. As your own faith grows, so will your ability to mediate God's acceptance and His power to meet every need. Only God can grant you the inner vision to see your loved one whole and complete in Christ, able to say *no* to the things that would destroy him.

Titus 2:11–12 promises, "For the grace of God that brings salvation has appeared to all men. It teaches us to say 'No' to ungodliness and worldly passions, and to live self-controlled, upright and godly lives in this present age."

Let us pray for such grace.

8

AIDS: Helping Them Live, Watching Them Die

This is perhaps the most difficult chapter to address to the family and friends of those who choose a homosexual lifestyle. Statistics indicate that of all the cases of full-blown Acquired Immune Deficiency Syndrome, upwards of eighty percent are gay males. There is hope for healing homosexual brokenness, but at this point there is no medical cure for the body that contracts AIDS. An understanding of the disease can help us understand the men and women who will become statistics and help us present Christ's love in a redeeming way.

There are actually three stages to this disease that has filled our world with fear. When a deadly virus, Human Immunodeficiency Virus, is detected in the blood system, the person is said to have tested HIV-positive. This does not mean the person has AIDS, only that he has been infected with the virus.

It may take as long as six months from the time the virus is introduced into the body before antibodies are detected. These antibodies are the indicator that blood banks look for in screening blood. Thus, a person could donate tainted blood during those twelve weeks and no one would be aware of it. Also, any sexual contact with another person during that period could pass on the virus.

Someone who tests positive could go many years with no obvious symptoms. In fact, he would not even know he had the virus unless he took a blood test to determine if antibodies were present.

A second stage of the disease is AIDS-Related Complex (ARC). This means an infected person has physical reactions less severe than full-blown AIDS but that may still be deadly. For many this brings the first realization they have been infected. Some people develop AIDS without any symptoms of ARC.

Some but not all of these symptoms include:

- A heavy cough that is not from smoking and lasts more than two weeks; also can be accompanied by fever and shortness of breath
- A severe weight loss in a short time
- Unexplained skin rashes
- Swollen glands in any part of the body
- Extreme tiredness, loss of appetite, dizziness or other flu-like symptoms that do not respond to over-the-counter medication
- Diarrhea that lasts for several weeks
- Any dramatic change in the motor or neurological functions of the body

The length of time that may lapse from infection to ARC is uncertain but could be as long as ten years. It is believed by most experts that anyone who comes down with ARC will eventually come down with AIDS.

AIDS Diseases

There are several diseases that can manifest in the body when a person is diagnosed with AIDS. Only when one of these diseases is present is the case reported to the Centers for Disease Control (C.D.C.) in Atlanta.

Three common diseases will lead to a full-blown AIDS diagnosis:

- Pneumocystis carinii pneumonia
- Dementia (upwards of sixty percent of AIDS patients have developed this condition as the disease progresses)
- Wasting Syndrome (severe unexplained weight loss).

It is not the virus itself that kills the patient but the breakdown of the immune system that leaves the body vulnerable to a number of opportunistic infections. When a case of AIDS is diagnosed, it generally means death within two years.

Theories on Transmission

Since 1981, when the first diagnosis of AIDS was made, the face of this disease has changed almost daily. It was thought originally that some HIV-positive persons might beat the death sentence and never develop full-blown AIDS. While current statements regarding the inevitability of progression to AIDS are still speculative, it appears that this might not be the case.

There was also speculation that transmission occurred only among homosexuals having sexual relations, intravenous drug users and hemophiliacs. Now we find the virus transmitted heterosexually through prostitutes, mothers with AIDS giving birth and blood transfusions. Extremely sensitive testing has also found the virus in low concentrations in tears and saliva. To this date, however, there is no data indicating it has ever been passed on from those particular fluids.

A statement from the 1988 position paper of the First Presbyterian Church in Hollywood includes a caution for caregivers: "Research on how AIDS is transmitted continues to be conducted. We must keep aware of developments in medical understanding of the contagiousness of HIV."

The Centers for Disease Control, which has been collecting information on the transmission of AIDS since 1981, reports that approximately five percent of persons with AIDS do not fall into any of the high-risk groups. They cannot identify how the person came into contact with the virus.

The standard resource for information on AIDS is the Surgeon General's Report, which is updated continually. It states, "AIDS is an infectious disease. It is contagious, but it cannot be spread in the same manner as a common cold or measles or chicken pox. It is contagious in the same way that sexually transmitted diseases, such as syphilis and gonorrhea, are contagious."

In that report Dr. C. Everett Koop estimated that 100 million people will die from AIDS by the end of the century. Other reports estimate that 250,000 Americans will die from AIDS by 1993. Whatever the totals, these are statistics that implant fear and prejudice into the hearts of millions.

Are Statistics Accurate?

It is unknown how many HIV-positive persons there are in the world because not everyone is tested. Even some who have been tested have been exposed too recently to develop antibodies and do not show the virus. One conservative estimate is currently more than two million cases in the United States. Given the inexorable progress of the disease, these all will eventually develop full-blown AIDS.

It is difficult to comprehend such high numbers. Although we read the increasing statistics, we tend to skim over these projections of loss of life—that is, until one of these statistics becomes a person we know and love.

HIV: What It Is, What It Does

The AIDS virus attacks a person's immune system and damages the ability of his body to fight off other diseases. The virus enters the body through some opening in the skin, external or internal, and finds its way to the white blood cells. These are called T-lymphocytes or T-cells and are in all human blood. They are the cells that produce the substances to attack and destroy any invading germs into the body.

The HIV (AIDS virus) seeks out this group of cells and attaches to them. This virus may remain dormant indefinitely, until the T-cells are activated to fight some type of infection in the body. At that point the HIV will reproduce itself and kill off the T-cells before they can do their job. The virus will continue to spread and destroy any T-cells in the body until there is no immune defense left.

It is not the AIDS virus that kills the person, but some disease that could have been combated by the T-lymphocytes if they were active in the blood as they are in healthy bodies.

It is important to realize that once the HIV enters the blood system it can be passed on to others, and that it never leaves the system.

The HIV is particularly deadly to the central nervous system and may go directly to the brain. It could take years to develop into a noticeable disease, but the Centers for Disease Control states that about ninety percent of those who die from HIV-related conditions are affected in their nervous systems to some degree.

Although this is a simplistic explanation of an extremely complicated disease, the important message is this: *There is no cure.*

What About Research?

While not every Christian may feel compelled to be involved on a one-to-one basis, every Christian can pray. Those who pray can also locate a group ministering to practical needs and even contribute financially. The 1989 walkathon for AIDS in San Francisco, attended by people from all walks of life, including Christians, raised one and a half million dollars. This money is needed to support research for new drugs as well as make existing medications available.

Currently six drugs are being used to help extend the lives of those with AIDS. These are the most promising of all that have been produced in recent years.

AZT: Currently the only FDA-approved drug licensed to treat HIV. It appears to slow the replication of HIV. The ill effects are damage to the bone marrow, and the fact that many patients cannot tolerate the drug physically.

ddI: About half as potent as AZT, with only one-tenth the toxicity. While testing is conducted, the manufacturer, Bristol-Myers, is making it available at no cost. If results are positive, it will probably replace AZT.

ddC: Powerful anti-viral properties, but highly toxic and cannot be tolerated for long periods. It is viewed as one to alternate with AZT.

Compound Q: Appears to attack and kill only HIV-infected cells, at least from early test-tube research. It has created a lot of excitement, but the results are far from conclusive.

Aerosolized Pentamidine: Appears most significantly to prevent pneumocystic carinii pneumonia, and has been licensed recently by the FDA for that purpose.

Ganciclovir: Has shown promise as a prevention against blindness caused by cytomegalovirus. This is one of the common complications of HIV infection.

119

As more discoveries are made each week, we should pray that God will bring the right combinations together to treat the various complications from HIV. Even if a drug were discovered today that could prevent the deadly virus from destroying the T-cells, those already infected make AIDS the "plague" of the century. Finding a cure will not change homosexual behavior, but it may prolong the lives of men and women until they can come to a personal relationship with the God of love.

Education: Who Is Responsible?

I have spoken with many people who still view AIDS as something that happens to homosexuals or drug addicts. The truth is, it can and does happen in Christian families, in churches across America and the world, and to individuals who might have committed adultery or had only one sexual encounter as long as ten years ago.

The rise in teenage HIV-positive statistics is alarming. The answer, according to many reports, is in education— by the printed page, classes and radio and television spots. This "education" tells how to engage in "safe sex"—let condoms become part of the standard dating kit and use sterile needles for drugs, for example.

The alarm has been sounded regarding AIDS, but I think the real plague is lack of moral teaching and examples by parents and educational leaders. AIDS, syphilis, gonorrhea and other sexually transmitted diseases are the fruit of a plague of national immorality. Unfortunately, AIDS is a deadly price to pay.

I believe sex education should start in the home, as soon as kids begin to ask where they came from. Children's books help answer questions on the most basic level and grow with the need to know. Parents themselves should become informed not only about the negative results of promiscuity but about the Scriptures that tell how God intended for sexual expression to enhance a marriage commitment.

Pre-teens and older teenagers should have straight talk about sex from their parents. They should not have to learn partial truths from their peers.

Sex is God's gift to us, but outside of marriage, according to the Bible, we are to abstain from sexual activity. Disease is just one of many reasons.

What About Children Who Have Experimented?

In *You Can Protect Yourself and Your Family from AIDS,* Clif Cartland, former publisher and editor-in-chief of *Family Life Today,* says: "Surveys are consistent in saying the following: Sexual intercourse is not uncommon among children as young as twelve years old. By the time young people reach the age of seventeen, more than half of them have had sexual intercourse."

Cartland discusses in depth the most current surveys of all types of sexual contact that teens and pre-teens have admitted to in confidential questionnaires.

In ages ranging from eight to eighteen, some sort of sexual experimentation has occurred that could transmit the AIDS virus in ways other than sexual intercourse. (Oral sex and hand manipulation of the genitals can be dangerous if there are cuts in the skin. The virus is alive in both semen and vaginal secretions as well as saliva.) Most teens were not aware they were at risk with this type of sexual activity.

The risk of AIDS increases with every new sexual encounter, because a person is exposed to every sexual partner that his or her partner has come in contact with for the past eight to ten years. The Surgeon General's Report recommends coming into marriage as a virgin and staying with one partner for a lifetime. In this age of promiscuity hardly anyone, male or female, qualifies for that standard. If your children are junior high age or older they should be told the risks and cautioned about activity. In loving them enough to discuss sexual issues you may never have to confront the tragic diagnosis of AIDS.

Not all persons with same-sex preference and sexual experience will come down with AIDS. The statistics are highest for gay men, although there are reported cases of lesbians contracting the disease. Numbers of gay men are sexually active, yet have not tested positive.

I had a face-to-face conversation recently with Steven, a friend of many years. We had not been in close contact for almost ten years, other than birthday and Christmas cards. After a short time of catching up on family, I asked the question most on my mind.

"Steven, have you gone for the AIDS test?" I watched his face for signs of stress or hesitancy.

"Yes." He paused. "And I really expected to test positive. I had prepared myself to hear the diagnosis." He grinned and shrugged. "It was negative."

"I'm glad, Steven. I pray for you a lot." I looked him in the eyes. "Has it changed your sexual behavior?"

"Some . . . but I'm not ever going to be celibate!"

I said simply, "I'll keep praying."

The Test . . . And Behavioral Changes

I polled an informal sampling of the gay men I knew to find out if taking the AIDS test had changed their sexual behavior.

I found that if they were not trying to serve God with their lives, their mentality tended to resemble a sexual roulette game they figured they could win with safe-sex precautions.

If they were active in their relationship with Christ and unmarried, they were resigned to a celibate life.

The truth about AIDS and homosexuality is that someone who is sexually active with a number of other people runs a high risk of being infected with the virus. Anyone who has ever been at risk should take the test to determine exposure. If the test is positive, a person can infect every sexual partner for the rest of his life.

Some gay men have told me they do not want to know if they have the virus and they refuse to take the test. This, they feel, is their moral right. It is another very good reason to educate children and teens, because their first or next sexual experience could be with someone afraid to find out if he has already been infected.

How AIDS Is Not Transmitted

According to the Surgeon General's Report, it is very difficult to become infected with the virus unless you are engaged in high-risk activity. I have read other material, however, that leaves many of us uneasy about that conclusion.

David Chilton, minister at Church of the Redeemer in Placerville, California, raises some very interesting questions in *Power in the Blood* . "One issue yet to be resolved," he writes, "is just how many different variations of the AIDS retrovirus actually exist." The National Cancer Institute has isolated at least eighteen different AIDS contagions.

Chilton also poses the question as to why several doctors who assert that the virus cannot be passed on by something so casual as drinking or eating after someone with AIDS would not do so themselves on a recent national television program. While not advocating panic, he calls for responsibility by telling people the truth: *We just do not know how the virus cannot be transmitted.*

Chilton's is one of many voices in the land crying out for a Christian response to AIDS, which includes a call for a return to biblical morality.

Many teenagers have told me, "If my parents would just explain why I shouldn't do something, then I could understand. All they ever tell me is not to do it." Perhaps an understanding of why will come with an understanding of the results of promiscuous sexual behavior.

For Those Already Positive

That there is no cure for AIDS falls heavily upon the heart of a parent or friend of someone who has already tested positive, someone for whom prevention is no longer an option. Parents may be presented with the revelation their child is gay at the same time they learn that child has AIDS.

AIDS, like every disease, doesn't happen just to the patient; it happens to everyone close to the patient. As a Christian parent in particular, you can do several things:

1. *Get more information.*

Testing HIV-positive doesn't mean someone has full-blown AIDS. Find out what each step means to you and to the person you love. (Resources are listed in Appendix III.)

2. *Don't panic.*

Assure him of your love and support. He was born your child and he will die your child.

3. *Find personal support.*

As volatile as the emotions of the AIDS patient are, the emotions of their parents will roller-coaster similarly through the weeks and months of this disease. There are several groups around the country that provide parental support. (Again, see Appendix III.)

4. *Refuse to live with guilt.*

Don't allow your mind to trap you into a "what-if" game. You cannot change the past, for yourself or your loved one. You can, however, help him to make the adjustment necessary to deal with the disease, and help him leave a legacy of courage for others.

5. *Help your child get right with God.*

Seek to restore him to a relationship with Christ if he is not currently in relationship with Him.

Jerry Arterburn in his book *How Will I Tell My Mother?* recounts that he had renewed his relationship to Jesus before he received his diagnosis and was somewhat prepared when the test came back positive. Jerry's parents assured him of their love and support.

Not all parents and friends have that grace initially, and only God can help them look beyond the diagnosis to the person facing death. Some parents, even Christian ones, absent themselves from the problem and abandon their children.

Jim adopted me as a substitute mom. He had come from a Christian family, attended a Christian college and become involved in a homosexual lifestyle. He had left his faith as a young man in his twenties and been estranged from his family for almost ten years. When he tested positive for AIDS he wanted to restore his relationship with his parents.

"I called them long distance," he told me. "I wept when I heard my mother's voice for the first time in ten years." Jim's voice broke with emotion. "I told her, 'Mom . . . Mom . . . I want to come home. I'm sorry for hurting you. I'm sorry for messing up my life. Mom, I've come back to Christ.' "

He told me there was only silence on her end. "Mom," he continued, "I don't have long to live. I have AIDS."

He told me it seemed like an eternity before she said at last, "You died to us ten years ago."

The line went dead and Jim never spoke to his mother again.

He became involved in his church, read my book *Long Road to Love* and decided to call me one night. We spoke every week for almost two years as his disease progressed. We talked about spiritual matters and prayed together, and he forgave his parents for their rejection.

The phone calls stopped several months ago, but I know I'll meet Jim in heaven someday.

Bob was also in his twenties. He shared his story with me on videotape with the hope it would help others.

Bob also grew up in a Christian family, attended a Christian college and had planned on full-time ministry. His parents had divorced just before his teenage years and Bob was sent to a Christian boarding school. An older student would sneak into Bob's room at night and fondle him while the other boys were asleep. Bob was afraid to tell anyone and lived with his secret for many years.

These experiences, together with his grief over his parents' divorce, created deep insecurities and negative self-esteem. Throughout his high school years he saw a lot of hypocrisy in the lives of his peers who were Christians but sexually immoral. Bob concluded that he must be homosexual since he had enjoyed the arousal of the earlier molestation.

He went to college fully intending to live out his Christianity and repress his homosexual feelings, but he decided the Bible was too rigid. He left the college and lived an active homosexual lifestyle for seven years. He was convinced there was no hope to change his orientation.

Because of his lack of closeness with his father, Bob had never felt free to share his homosexual orientation with him. He did tell his mother and siblings about his choice when he left college and asked them not to inform his dad.

Through a series of spiritual confrontations Bob returned to his faith in Christ and was given the hope that Jesus would restore him in every way, including a relationship with a wife and children. He was excited about serving God. He decided to take a responsible step toward recovery and took the AIDS test.

The test came back positive. Two years later Bob developed full-blown AIDS.

He has shared the diagnosis with his family, including his dad. They are supporting him emotionally. He also travels with groups around the country to share with churches the miracle of God's work in his life. Bob has accepted God's sovereignty over this disease and is looking to Him for a complete healing, either here or in heaven. Bob says he has found support and restoration within the Body of Christ, and he is content to leave the future in God's hands.

A final experience was recounted in the January/February 1989 issue of *A Call to Evangelical Action*. It tells of Keith and how his parents responded to his involvement in homosexuality and a recent diagnosis of AIDS.

Keith's Christian parents had to work through their shock and disappointment. Keith tells of having been introduced to the homosexual lifestyle at church camp as a junior high student. He struggled silently with his confusion and feelings for twelve years. He felt God's call on his life and responded by attending Bible college. No longer engaging in sexual activity, he felt God was working a deep healing in his life. The attraction to fellows was not as strong as it had been in high school.

Then Keith gave blood for a Red Cross blood drive. The report they gave him took him by surprise. Although he had been sexually pure for several years, he had been exposed already to the virus.

Keith's family and fellow students at Bible school stood by him with encouragement. Now he shares his story whenever the opportunity is given. He also carries a letter he received from a female friend of the family:

> After hearing about your diagnosis, I was sure it was a mistake. Only evil, wicked people get AIDS. But you are neither evil nor wicked. People who get AIDS deserve what they get. But you don't deserve it. All

of my ideas about AIDS have been blown apart by
you because you are a person, you are my friend. You
aren't just a nameless face. I know you . . . and I
know your family.

That young woman took the first step in understanding
and overcoming fear. Despite the statistics, she gave Bob
encouragement to live. She gave the faceless monster, the
victim of AIDS, a name. She called him friend.

9

The Right Hand of Fellowship

My clock radio clicked on at 6:30 A.M. I had forgotten it was Sunday morning and I could sleep an extra hour. I rolled over, my arm extended to push the "off" button, when I heard the talk-show host make this statement:

"All of the evangelical fundamentalist Christians resent what we're doing with this walkathon to raise money to combat AIDS. In their homophobic narrowmindedness, they say that this is God's judgment on homosexuals and they should be left to die."

I sat up in bed and reached for the phone, my extra hour of sleep now forgotten. *How dare he classify all born-again Christians as homophobic, uncaring individuals*, I thought. *And finding a cure for a disease is certainly not the same as condemning an action that spreads it!*

I dialed the station and waited patiently on the line for twenty minutes. When I heard his voice telling me I was on the air I worded my response carefully so he would not cut me off before I had made my point.

"How can you make such a broad statement that all evangelical Christians who oppose homosexual activity on a biblical basis are automatically homophobic and hate the victims of a deadly disease?" I paused. "I am a born-again Christian and the Bible says that the act of homosexuality is a sin, but I certainly support any method of trying to find a cure for the disease. AIDS is a deadly result of bad choices, but just because we're Christians we don't hate those who made the choices, and neither does God." The line clicked and went dead.

I listened to my radio as he mumbled that perhaps he was too inclusive when he said *all* evangelicals were narrowminded and hated gays. He ended his comments with, "But I'll tell you one thing. That lady is in the minority of fundamentalists!"

I didn't have the chance to dialogue with him, but my heart is burdened that he is able to affect the thinking of people on the West Coast by a few "fundy-phobic" statements! He was basing his belief about all Christians upon the actions of a few outspoken Christian fundamentalists who are active in opposing legislative measures that would grant minority status to the gay community.

The argument continued in my head about the unfairness of such judgments as I hopped into the shower. Then I realized something: The response is the same with the Christian community that tends to lump all homosexuals and persons with AIDS into the same basket! God wants us to respond to people, not to behavior patterns or diseases that result from them.

The Church's Greatest Challenge

When the AIDS epidemic hit America, I believe there was a unique challenge given to the Church of Jesus Christ. This is not just to respond with compassion to these individuals, but to impact a community with a clear message of reconciliation. The challenge is stronger today than ever.

One such group responding is ARM (AIDS Resource Ministry). This is a branch of Desert Stream Ministries in Santa Monica, California. It is directed by Jonathan Hunter, who is a caring and compassionate man. He is also HIV-positive.

Jonathan was once a top international model, addicted to drugs and sex. He had a near-fatal overdose that got his attention and caused him to turn to God. He became involved with Desert Stream and as men around him began to die from AIDS he felt compelled to minister to them. Especially after testing positive himself, he felt an urgency to train volunteers to reach out to those on the AIDS ward. The ministry of ARM is practical: cooking meals, cleaning, shopping and all the things that need to be done. Yet, as Jonathan said in a recent interview, "We can't neglect the spiritual aspect."

Hunter trains volunteers at conferences that last two and a half days. They receive intensive instruction in the practical how-to's, as well as insights on how to share Christ.

ARM currently has three aspects to its ministry:

• A support group for persons who have AIDS or who have tested positive
• A support group for parents and loved ones

• A core of about fifteen people who visit, help and comfort AIDS patients.

Information on contacting ARM is in Appendix III.

ARM is one of many of the ex-gay ministries around the world that is active in responding to the disease of AIDS. Exodus International has a growing list of groups that are establishing homes for the care of patients and their families.

What About Mainline Churches?

Almost every denomination has now established a statement of response to the AIDS situation. Many of the larger churches are working at training those who feel urged to do more.

Yet we still hear of stories like the one reported in the October 1988 *Moody Monthly*. M. F. Brucker told how a woman called the pastor of the largest church in her Midwestern city.

"My son is dying of AIDS. Will you please come and pray with him?"

"Yes," said the senior pastor.

"Oh, thank you, thank you," the woman sobbed. "You're the fifth church I've called."

"What happened to the others?"

"Two hung up on me. One outright refused. And one didn't answer at all."

As unsettling as that story is, there are hundreds to match it. Responding to the need is overwhelming. With so much fear and misinformation, many wonder if it is safe to come anywhere near an AIDS patient. The irony is that you cannot tell at first glance if people have AIDS and possibly come in contact with them every day.

The answer to this dilemma is to find out what can be done and to do it. Wisdom must be exercised when ministering to those with AIDS, and protection taken when coming in contact with any body fluids. I believe our commission is to minister with the same attitude of compassion that Christ exhibited when He healed the sick. We are His ministers to the diseased and broken humanity of this century.

It seems to me that throughout Scripture Christ first met the physical need, then addressed the spiritual condition of the person. The Church must begin now to meet the physical needs of AIDS patients. Within a few short years, every person in the United States will know someone who has or is dying from this disease.

Doug Houck (Metanoia Ministry in Seattle) was quoted in the same issue of *Moody Monthly* as saying, "Most of the help for AIDS victims is coming from the gay community and the government. The current church response is one of helplessness."

It is apparent that from New York to San Francisco, in large towns and in small, the gay community has developed a network of support for those who come down with AIDS. It is friend caring for friend, as daycare facilities and hospital space are increasingly limited in their capacity to provide care.

City, county and state funds and groups are stretched to their limits and this disease has only just begun to take its toll on the men and women in America. The millions of dollars allocated by the government will not be adequate to meet the need. In the July 14, 1989, edition of the San

Francisco *Chronicle*, Randy Shilts lists new statistics on AIDS that cause health care professionals to shudder. "It took six and a half years of the epidemic to get the first 50,000 cases in America. It took only 18 months to get the second 50,000 cases. Now, the C.D.C. calculates less than 12 months to get the next 50,000, and less than 10 months for the 50,000 after that."

There is already a shortage of professional nurses and physicians and the bulk of care will fall increasingly on family and friends. There are about 5,000 treatment programs nationwide, with limited space, and most have waiting lists of several months. In some areas county homes are provided only for persons in the last stages of the disease. Often there is no one, from either the family or the gay community, able to spend the last days with these people.

This is one of many opportunities for the Church body to reach out and express God's love. The Church needs to be at the front lines to bind up the wounded. We must help them live, until they die. As individuals, we can make an impact on the lives of a few; as congregations or entire denominations, we can touch hundreds. This means starting new programs and joining together with existing works, both secular and Christian.

Here are five suggestions to help your church family get started.

Steps for the Church Fellowship

1. *Educate the congregation.*
This is the first—and perhaps most important—step. It requires the leadership of the church to become knowl-

edgeable about topics of homosexuality and AIDS. It involves moving beyond the biblical teachings of sin and obtaining a working knowledge of current psychological approaches to the treatment of the whole person, not just one phase of behavior.

It requires also that the pastor become a clearinghouse of sorts to determine from reliable sources what is fact and fiction, truth and rumor, and then communicate such information from the pulpit. It also means having resources available for church members to do research themselves.

Hank, a pastor in Kansas, was catapulted into an AIDS-education program when three young men in his congregation tested positive. They were all from Christian families and all had worked in the youth or music ministry since they were teenagers. They weren't statistics from the New York *Times*; they were sons of deacons and Sunday school teachers.

Hank told me that until this happened it was easy to ignore the statistics, and even to preach condemnation of homosexuals. When AIDS had a face he knew and loved, Hank was forced to view homosexual behavior as just one of many sins. He learned to speak to the consequences of that sinful behavior, and to reach out with compassion as he held the hand of each of those boys who died within two years of each other. Hank got educated firsthand and his church now has an outreach called His Hand Extended.

As part of the education of the congregation, a statement of policy should be established for responding to persons with AIDS. This should include the handling of infants or children with AIDS, and how they can receive ministry without placing others at risk. This policy should cover the baptism of adults or those who might possibly work in kitchen areas.

Two such churches with established position papers are the First Presbyterian Church of Hollywood and the Philadelphia Church in Chicago. They provide specific guidelines so parishioners will know how to respond, and so the person with AIDS will know what to expect from the church. Both sides can benefit from such knowledgeable and compassionate planning.

2. *Offer tangible assistance.*

Many churches have responded to the poor of their community by establishing food banks or clothing banks available for urgent-need cases or year-round ministry, depending upon the size of the fellowship.

A similar resource could be developed for outreach to the person with AIDS. Perhaps seniors could become involved with cooking meals, driving to doctor appointments, shopping or just visiting and sharing with those who cannot get out of their homes or hospital wards.

Singles or young marrieds could become involved with cleaning, laundry or light jobs around the home for those who are too weak to care for themselves.

As the cases increase, there will also be a growing need for housing or short-term board and care, which the Church can assist in providing.

At the very least, finances can be designated to help support existing works, both Christian and secular.

3. *Help the family of the person with AIDS.*

Families need encouragement and acceptance as much as the person with AIDS. The pastor should institute support groups for parents, spouses, siblings, any who are living through this disease with their loved ones. If the church is limited by its size from offering such support, then Christian counseling services in the area or community mental health agencies are available resources.

Christian counseling services often charge on a sliding scale according to the income of the family. They provide a confidential sounding board with biblical foundations to gird up the entire family unit.

I have found these counseling agencies most valuable when the psychological issues involve more than I am trained to deal with.

In addition to working with family members in tangible ways, the Church is called upon to help them deal with the emotional turmoil that results from finding out a loved one is homosexual, let alone diagnosed with AIDS.

An excellent resource for equipping the nonprofessional helper is Dr. Timothy Foster's book *Called to Counsel*. He provides information on what to do and not to do when assisting the family and in personal counseling. The primary goals should be to bring family members to a place of reconciliation with one another and to assist in the restoration process.

The family needs not only someone to listen, but to have the confidence that what is said will not be repeated. Dr. Foster says, "Never break confidences; never talk behind the person's back. Your commitment to that person extends more than to just a certain time period." Families need to know you support them in the time of crisis and will not exploit them in public.

When the family is hurting, don't hesitate to suggest professional therapy if you see that the problems are beyond your ability as pastor or lay counselor. They should always be assured of your prayers and friendship, but often the family interaction is too complicated to be resolved with other than professional help.

The parents who are faced with sons or daughters with AIDS deal with a variety of emotions. I talked with one mom who was somewhat of a guilt sponge. She was sure she had made major mistakes in how she raised her son. She felt guilty that she was so disconnected she had not even realized he struggled with homosexuality. She felt even more guilty because he had died from AIDS.

It was just a few days before his death that Mark had made his peace with God and confessed "all" to his mother. She had not had time to adjust to the death of her son, let alone the knowledge of the lifestyle that exposed him to the virus. She found some comfort in Mark's last words:

"Mom, you did the best you could with what you had. Nothing I've done is your fault. God has forgiven me . . . and you."

She has a long way to go on her journey of healing, and some of her questions have no easy answers. She still wonders how AIDS can happen in a Christian family, and her husband asks how a son of his could have been homosexual. The Church needs to be ready with comfort when such questions are clothed in grief.

Many Christian families don't know how they will tell their church, their friends and their neighborhoods if a child does come home to spend the last months of life.

I was speaking at a women's retreat and showing a video of an interview I had done with an AIDS patient named Bob. He is a Christian and has been diagnosed recently with full-blown AIDS. The interview was about an hour long and as it played I watched the faces of the women in the room.

One woman had tears streaming down her cheeks. She was biting her lower lip in an attempt to control her emotions. After the video was finished most of the women filed from the room. I walked over and sat beside Myrtle and put my hand on her shoulder.

"Are you O.K.?" I asked.

She shook her head. The tears streaked through her makeup. She tried to brush them away. "I can't talk to anyone . . . not even my church." She looked directly into my eyes. "I lost my son to AIDS in December. . . . No one knows."

I wrapped my arms around her and just held her while she cried.

"It's O.K. to cry," I whispered. "Jesus knows . . . and He won't betray your secret."

Myrtle and I kept in touch during the retreat and I promised to pray for her as she dealt with the grief of losing her son. She still deals with the frustration of a church family that cannot be told because they would condemn.

One mother told me that she was pained not only at finding out her son had AIDS, but more pained at how people responded when she wanted to help him have a yard sale so he could move home. When some of the neighbors found out he had AIDS, they refused to come anywhere near the sale and actively boycotted it.

Families need comfort when hostility and fear bring isolation.

Families also need direction when their financial resources are being tapped. Some parents become the sole support for their children as the disease progresses. As the active cases of AIDS continue to escalate, medical insurance and space available in hospitals will diminish, even for those who can afford the high costs.

In July 1989 new statistics were released by the C.D.C. that place active cases at just over 100,000. If the infected population is anywhere near the projected two or three million who have not yet come down with full-blown AIDS, then it is only a matter of time until every church will have one or more families dealing with this epidemic. We need to be prepared to help them.

4. *Help the helper.*

One of the most important areas of knowledge for anyone who wants to help—individual or church—is to know your limitations. Caring for the terminally ill can be draining physically and shattering emotionally when the patients die. It is good to have available resources to help the helper deal with the issues of death. It is good to have a sounding board of leadership personnel to whom the helpers are accountable. One resource recommends that helpers work in groups of two so that the burden can be shared and the emotions discussed as they come up, rather than be put off until a scheduled time. The helpers may identify so strongly with the person who has the disease that they go through the stages of grief also.

Ruth found this to be true. She was a co-worker of mine for many years until her retirement at 65. She still wanted to help people so she joined a hospice group with the county. She described the long weeks of training and evaluation prior to being assigned a patient. She could not understand initially why it took so long to "get on with it." She was forced to deal with her feelings about death, work out solutions of counsel and plan how she would deal with that first death of a client.

When that day came, she knew why the training had been so intensive. The loss was as if it had been a family member. Ruth recalled to me the importance then of having someone she could talk with and who could help her work through the grief. County hospice workers are required to attend meetings and talk about their feelings, and are limited to the number of patients they take at a time. It is all volunteer work and is not associated with a church.

If the Church is to be effective in this area of ministry, it also will need a place of refuge for its own healing of helpers.

5. *Plan for hospital visitation.*

Jonathan Hunter, director of ARM, states in his January 1986 newsletter that "if you are visiting someone in a hospital, know the rules and regulations of the hospital, which serve to protect the patient." He offers several guidelines:

Do not walk in unannounced. Go through proper channels, such as the chaplain. Let it be known that you are interested in helping with visits.

Be sure of your own motives for visitation. Don't go in with the intent of "leading this sinner to Jesus." He may already be a Christian. One article I read suggested, "If you are visiting someone with lung cancer, it doesn't help him to count up how many cigarettes he smoked in his life."

Be a friend. You can share your belief in Christ and His love for AIDS patients, but don't push your beliefs on them. They should see by your actions something that would attract them to personal faith in Christ.

Keep your promises. If you say you will return, do so. If they are well enough to leave the hospital, make them aware of support groups. And promise them only things you are ready and willing to supply.

Don't give false hope for healing. While Christ is the Healer, we should keep in mind that emotional and spiritual healing are God's priority. Do pray with and for them, but help them seek the Healer, not just a healing.

Other Victims of AIDS

It is no longer just single men and women who, by their lifestyles, contract the disease and involve church families.

We have all heard of cases of transmittal through blood transfusions. They are victims not of behavior choices but of a plague.

It was reported in the San Francisco *Chronicle* in July 1989 that there are now more than 3,000 babies who have been born with the AIDS virus. They are often placed in foster homes because their mothers are not able, or do not want, to care for them. If children follow the current trend from the time of infection to manifestation, they will not live to see their tenth birthdays.

A recent report from the C.D.C. says the cases of AIDS in teenagers have risen dramatically. Teens are surpassed only by black IV drug-users as a high-risk group.

What About Precautions?

Those with obvious occupations of high risk are health care workers, lab technicians and physicians. Increasingly, there are other occupations being touched by risk of AIDS infection.

In California several police officers have been bitten or

scratched by people with AIDS. The warning has gone out that anyone who comes in contact with the blood of another individual is at risk.

Almost every dentist and hygienist now uses gloves and a mask when treating patients. It was a strange experience after twenty years with the same dentist to have the staff suddenly look as if they were entering a surgery room.

Another career at risk I had not considered until recently was that of the mortician. Last year when I experienced the loss of my mother and stepfather within weeks of one another, I decided to ask how AIDS has affected morticians' performances in dealing with the deceased. I spoke with Lee, who had been in the business in that small town for almost thirty years. He expressed grave concern.

"You don't have the case history on everyone who comes here, and I know of at least one case where blood splattered into the eyes of a worker. He later tested positive." Lee shook his head. "Even in a town as small as ours, you can't afford to take a chance."

Towns large and small are affected in the area of health care work. Cari, a nurse who attends our church, shared with me recently that within the past few months she has been accidentally stuck with a needle twice while caring for patients. Each time brought new panic because she didn't know if the patients were carrying the AIDS virus. Cari's experiences turned out happily. Her patients were HIV-negative.

For at least one health care worker in San Francisco, even with all the precautions involved in changing needles, the virus was transmitted by an accidental prick.

There is no complete guarantee of safety. I even heard of another case of AIDS that had been contracted in a tattoo parlor because the needle was not disinfected.

I spoke with Tim who resides in a group home with five other men. Tim has had full-blown AIDS for one year. I asked him what special measures were taken as far as food or eating utensils in a community living area.

"We label the food in the refrigerator and keep it separate, although there is no risk of transferring the virus through touching the items." He paused. "I keep my drinking glass and personal hygiene items separate, too, even though there is no evidence that I could transmit the virus through them. I couldn't live with myself if that ever happened. I would rather err on the side of caution."

Tim pointed out that the person with AIDS can at times experience great weakness and not be able to do anything for himself. He says that this is one way Christians can minister to specific needs—actually help feed the person with AIDS.

We talked more about the responsibility of a person with AIDS to do what is necessary not to infect others, intentionally or unintentionally. Tim shared that his deepest feelings of regret are regarding those men with whom he had sexual contact before he took the AIDS test. He lives with the knowledge that he is responsible for passing on the virus to others.

I asked him, "Why did you wait so long to take the test? And what would you say to someone who is homosexual and has not yet been tested?"

Tim's reply still rings in my memory.

"I was afraid to take the test. I didn't want to know if I

was sick because I knew there wasn't any cure. Finally I felt God was telling me I needed to be responsible for my future. I had to take the test."

Tim repeated my question. "What would I tell someone? I'd say get the test. Ignoring it won't make AIDS go away. The fear of knowing is overwhelming, but living with the knowledge that you may have caused someone else's death is worse."

Another part of our Christian responsibility is to pray that the high-risk population across America and around the world will have the courage to find out if their behavior has made them HIV-positive. There needs to be, as Tim told me, "a responsibility for the future."

Our response needs to be one of compassion and love, and yet with responsible precautions to prevent contact with body fluids from a person with AIDS.

Gloves are a good precautionary measure—though the people who are suffering from the isolation that AIDS can bring need physical contact at times. Shaking hands and giving a person a hug won't pass on the AIDS virus, but if you are going to touch any body fluids, gloves are an important choice. Caring for a person, for instance, who has pneumonia and is vomiting or has diarrhea also necessitates gloves. Feeding a person with AIDS, however, does not necessarily mean you will come in contact with any body fluids. Also, keep the dishes separate and wash them in hot soapy water.

This knowledge should not incite fear in reaching out with compassion, but should encourage responsible handling of items that might be infected with the virus. It also can give us the liberty to provide what the person with

AIDS needs most—a warm hug and lots of prayer. That's friendship and godly compassion meeting real and tangible needs.

Qualifications for Workers

What does it take to help these suffering men and women? A helper should:

1. *Be full of caring and compassion.*

Second Corinthians 1:3–4 says:

> Praise be to the God and Father of our Lord Jesus Christ, the Father of compassion and the God of all comfort, who comforts us in all our troubles, so that we can comfort those in any trouble with the comfort we ourselves have received from God.

Perhaps this is why the majority of nonprofessional helpers for people with AIDS are those from the gay community who have lost friends and loved ones from this disease. Many themselves are also carrying the virus and learning to live with its limitations.

A second group of helpers comes from the families of people who have died with AIDS. Many times it is this outreach that helps them work through the grief of their loss.

Together with the above groups are the Christians who want to make a difference spiritually for those who have tested positive. A majority of the ministry outreaches are staffed by people who have also left the homosexual lifestyle and want to share with others that message of hope for spiritual healing.

As the statistics soar in the years ahead, this call for compassion and comfort will be answered by the mass of people not yet touched by any of the above situations. Every Christian will need to resolve his part in taking the love of Christ to dying men and women. We must pray for that compassion to be born in us now so that we will respond as Christ would do if He were here in the flesh.

2. *Have a desire to help others.*

> Let us not become weary in doing good, for at the proper time we will reap a harvest if we do not give up. Therefore, as we have opportunity, let us do good to all people, especially to those who belong to the family of believers. Galatians 6:9–10

When we truly desire to help hurting people, God will provide the opportunity for us to do so. I have already mentioned the emotional stress and physical weariness that can burden the caretaker of a person with AIDS.

It is good to pace yourself, allow for times of relaxation and have a person or group you can interact with to lift the pressure of the burden. The harvest of reward in helping others is most often the development of Christian character.

A desire to help people means that we set aside our judgments, present Christ's compassion through our action and, if given permission, pray with them.

If they are not part of the family of believers, perhaps you will be given the privilege of being the first to welcome them home. If they are believers, you may be part of their strengthening of faith as they prepare for their final journey Home.

3. *Be willing to deal with the fear of disease being transmitted.*
God speaks to the fear of disease in Psalm 91:3, 5–6:

Surely he will save you from the fowler's snare and
from the deadly pestilence. . . . You will not fear the
terror of night, nor the arrow that flies by day, nor the
pestilence that stalks in the darkness, nor the plague
that destroys at midday.

Fear can paralyze the outreach of any church or group of
individuals within the church fellowship. It is information
and knowledge about those things we fear (homosexuality
and AIDS) that can help us overcome any hesitance in
reaching out to minister God's healing grace.

I believe God will honor His Word in providing protection as wise and proper precautions are taken when it
might be necessary to come in contact with body fluids.
And there are many areas of care that do not put the
caretaker at risk at all.

A couple of years ago I had an experience that helped
me understand the helplessness of being around a disease
like AIDS. I have a friend, Rose, who is in her middle
thirties. She was diagnosed with Lou Gehrig's disease,
which attacks the nervous system and destroys the mus-
cles. I have watched her deteriorate from healthy vitality—
she used to backpack and bicycle with me—to a weakened
condition that requires 24-hour care, including feeding her
and helping her to move to a wheelchair so she can have
a change of scenery.

Because of my love for Rose, I wanted to help her. I
wanted to take her places and do things for her. Although
we never talked about it, I knew it was difficult for her to
have to be dependent upon others to do the things she
once did for herself.

I lived silently with the pain of losing a friend to that

fatal disease and, although it wasn't contagious, the fear of each visit's being the last actually kept me away longer each time. I did not want to live her pain, or see the effect the disease was having on her husband and children. I did not want to hurt, or see her hurt, when there was nothing I could do except hold her and pray for a healing that did not seem to be happening in her physical body. It became easier to send cards than to experience the pain. It was hard, but I had to overcome that sense of helplessness.

I think being around persons with AIDS can be like that. It is not always the fear of the disease itself, but the fear of caring and losing that stops us. Here, too, we can be enriched by the courage of those who live with AIDS; they have lessons to teach us. It is impossible to share intimately with people and not become emotionally attached. This is where grief counseling and hospice training will prove to be beneficial.

This disease will come near to us all. The fear of it can be more deadly to the soul than the disease is to the body. As we extend the right hand of fellowship, that hand may bring spiritual healing and reconciliation to the person with AIDS. If we fail to reach out because of our fear, we become ministers of death instead of life. In 1 John 4:18 we read, "There is no fear in love. But perfect love drives out fear, because fear has to do with punishment. The man who fears is not made perfect in love."

Let's ask God to perfect us in love so that we can reach others with His love.

4. *Be willing to listen.*

I've heard it said that the greatest need any person has is for someone really to listen to him. If that is true, and I believe it is, then the family of God should learn how to do it well.

A major element of listening is hearing what is not said, as much as what is said. A natural tendency is to make quick judgments or offer solutions to situations before we are asked. As Christians offering the right hand of fellowship, we should listen with a sympathetic ear, such as is described in 1 Peter 3:8: "Finally, all of you, live in harmony with one another; be sympathetic, love as brothers, be compassionate and humble."

To be willing to listen means to set aside quality time and invest a gift of caring in the life of someone else. It means to be ready to take a fresh look at the age-old problem of sin, and not automatically hit someone in the head with spiritual laws and commandments.

Being willing to listen is the first step of a journey you may take with a stranger, and find you have a brother. Many who are living and dying with AIDS are very much a part of the family of God.

5. *Be willing to be a friend.*

There are volumes written on the finer qualities of friendship, most of them stirring up deep emotions in us or at least a knowing smile of remembrance. We have moved beyond the Peanuts version of "A friend is someone who likes you," to a deeper understanding that to have friends, you must yourself become friendly. Friendship never just happens; it is chiseled out of busy work schedules, inconvenient telephone calls, sharing pain and victories and a deep commitment to caring.

The type of friendship called for in reaching out to homosexuals with AIDS has an additional facet that Jesus talked about in Matthew 25:37–40. He said, "Then the righteous will answer him, 'Lord, when did we see you . . a stranger and invite you in, or needing clothes, and clothe you? When did we see you sick or in prison and go to visit you?' The King will reply, 'I tell you the truth, whatever you did for one of the least of these brothers of mine, you did for me.' "

To be representatives of Jesus to a world that feels rejection and abandonment by men and God is a privilege and a command.

Jesus' own words tell us that the quality of true friendship is found in meeting tangible needs and going to visit those who cannot visit in return.

When we are committed to being this type of friend, we will earn the right to share deeper truths about how to live out a relationship with Jesus Christ.

Several years ago, I wrote a quote in the front of my Bible. I believe it holds true for a church that would welcome the broken, the hurting and rejected—those strangers in a Christian land: "People won't care how much you know until they know how much you care."

Let's meet the challenge with hand and heart extended.

Appendix I

Questions and Answers: Because You Asked

A phone call shattered the stillness of the midnight hour. I was half-asleep as I reached for the phone, mumbled, "Hello?" and glanced at the digital numbers reading 12:45 A.M.

"Hello." A feminine voice hesitated. "Did I wake you? You don't know me, but I just finished reading your book."

"Oh, that's nice." I sat up in bed. "Where are you calling from? You sound long distance."

"Illinois. Listen, I don't want to disturb you but I've got to know something. How are you doing today? Are you still straight? I mean, does it really work for you now?"

I flipped on my light. "That's a lot of questions rolled into one. Let me tell you that, yes, God is faithful to me and I continue to grow in His Word daily. There have been times of struggle, especially at first, but I can tell you that I am very much straight and that God's Word works for me and for hundreds of others that I am in contact with regularly."

"Are you ever tempted?" the voice asked.

"If you mean to sin, sure. Everyone has temptations. But I can tell you for sure, I'm not tempted ever to go back to a homosexual lifestyle."

The conversation continued on into the morning hours. This woman, like so many others, needed the assurance that it was possible to keep growing. It has been more than thirteen years since I recommitted my life to Christ. One thing I am even more confident of now is that Philippians 1:6 is a firm foundation: "Being confident of this, that he who began a good work in you will carry it on to completion until the day of Christ Jesus."

Over the past several years of counseling by mail, sending out questionnaires and responding to phone calls from across the nation, I have found a number of questions asked repeatedly. This section of the book is reserved for addressing those questions.

The most frequently asked is: "Are you the person on the front cover of *Long Road to Love?*" I chuckle as I respond, "No, that's probably some sweet pastor's wife in middle America who would be embarrassed if she knew her photo was on a book to minister to homosexuals."

I wish every question were as simple to answer. The calls and letters I receive are from hurting people, some on the verge of suicide, some in prison, some in the ministry, but all looking for a ray of hope to help them or their loved one overcome homosexuality.

I pray that you, the family and friends and loved ones of

people who struggle with homosexuality and AIDS, will find that hope as well.

Helping Others

Q. I just found out my brother is gay. I don't know how to communicate with him now. Everything I find in the library says this is a normal lifestyle. Where can I find the truth about this issue?

A. First, let me ask this: Does your brother claim a personal faith in Christ? If so, then perhaps you can show him such verses as Romans 1 and 1 Corinthians 6:9–11. These will not only give God's perspective on homosexuality but offer him hope for change. If he is not confessing Jesus Christ as his Savior, then you should pray for him to know God's love in a personal way.

Your brother needs to be able to agree that God's Word is truth and that, as 2 Timothy 3:16–17 says, "All Scripture is God-breathed and is useful for teaching, rebuking, correcting and training in righteousness, so that the man of God may be thoroughly equipped for every good work." What is truth will be in agreement with the Bible, and only the Holy Spirit can deal with the hearts of men. Just keep loving your brother, and let him know that God loves him, too, but wants to change his life so that he can become all that God intended for him to become.

Q. I have a daughter in the lifestyle. How can I cope with my own emotions and try to help her? How should I treat her friend?

A. First, remember: *You* are the only one *you* can change. Obtain support while you are learning to cope with this new information. I recommend a support group for parents, if one exists in your area. If not, contact Exodus International and get an address for correspondence with other parents.

You might also benefit from counseling with a pastor or a Christian therapist. If you don't know whom to call try the yellow pages of your phone directory.

You might also find a trusted Christian friend to share with and to support you in praying for your daughter.

Don't try to "fix" her, unless she asks you for help. You should try to keep the doors of communication open.

As to how you should treat her "friend," that is a difficult question. I recommend extending the love of God to her as you would your own daughter. If they come for visits that involve overnight accommodations, I recommend treating them the same as you would a heterosexual unmarried couple: no sleeping in the same room. Be open about the standards you wish to uphold in your Christian home. Be sure you make it clear that you do not condone homosexual behavior, but that you do love and accept them.

Q. From a pastor: How can I love men and women involved in the bondage of homosexuality in a way to be of real help to them?

A. I think loving them in a real way means to make clear to them that you accept them as valuable human beings, even though you do not accept homosexual behavior. Loving means to distinguish between harmful and healthy choices and to encourage people to make positive choices. Loving acceptance will do more to produce change than a hundred sermons on the abominations of homosexual behavior. Work at establishing a friendship, and don't be afraid to share some of your struggles.

Q. From a Christian counselor: How can I let the homosexual know he is loved, yet help him realize that his sinful behavior is offensive to God?

A. Communicating genuine love involves acceptance of that person, not just words. I feel that in the context of friendship you can share what Scripture has to say about sexual responsibility. Don't just focus in on homosexuality. A section of Scripture like Ephesians 5:3 could be shared: "But among you there must not be even a hint of sexual immorality, or of any kind of impurity, or of greed, because these are improper for God's holy people."

Our message must be that Christianity involves the total person, not just his sexual behavior.

Thought Life

Q. A frequent question from both men and women: Could you give me some help on how to fight the battle with my fantasy life? Is masturbation a sin?

A. Romans 12:2 says, "Do not conform any longer to the pattern of this world, but be transformed by the renewing of your mind." This is one place where struggle takes place. To renew your mind you must make conscious choices to think differently. Philippians 4:8 says, "Finally, brothers, whatever is true, whatever is noble, whatever is right, whatever is pure, whatever is lovely, whatever is admirable—if anything is excellent or praiseworthy—think about such things."

It takes a conscious choice to refuse to think about things that would cause emotions to arise that could lead to sinful behavior. In 2 Corinthians 10:5 we read, "We demolish arguments and every pretension that sets itself up against the knowledge of God, and we take captive every thought to make it obedient to Christ." This doesn't happen overnight, but to control your fantasy life means to reprogram how and what you meditate on each day.

The question of masturbation is not whether or not it is a sin but whether or not it drives you closer to God and helps you live a disciplined life. The body and the mind are fantastic creations of almighty God and work together. They create emotions that will lock us into behavior patterns for good or bad. The problem I see with masturbation is that you "picture" events or persons real or imagined that create sexual attraction to certain types of relationships. Your memory doesn't know if you have actually experienced a sexual encounter or just imagined it, but will store up the emotion for later recall and can trigger desire in your thoughts. This is why it is important to work on the reprogramming of your thought life with Scriptures, so that your behavior will be the result of godly thinking.

Q. From a twenty-year-old man in the Midwest: You told me not to buy into the label of "gay." Does that mean you think I might not be that much of a homosexual?

A. Often, as we go through puberty, we experience crushes and strong same-sex attractions. Part of this is a normal child-development process. We look for heroes and successful role models who can inspire us to achieve our potential. It may be that our peers will label us "fag" or "gay" because we admire the same sex. During this confusing time in our growth, we may begin to think we are gay. I feel that twenty is far too young to decide you are locked into a lifestyle without possibility of change.

I would recommend counseling on ways to affirm your male role. Do some study on the development of teenagers and pre-adult growth, and submit your sexuality to God.

Even if you have acted out your fantasy with another male, that doesn't mean you are homosexual. You were created by God to be a man, to grow and bring glory to your Creator. I think you will find as you develop positive relationships with men and women within the church setting that you will be more comfortable with the qualities God has given you. Remember, caring and tenderness are not strictly feminine attributes. These qualities can mature with you and one day make you a very special husband and father. If you must take a label, let it be that of a Christian man, and learn to be all that His label says you are.

Demons and Deliverance

Q. I am married, but still struggle with unnatural desires. Do I need deliverance?

A. You touch on several issues here. Being married, of course, is not a guarantee of heterosexuality. The struggle with "unnatural desires" could come from several things. If you are still in contact with former lovers, or cherish memories of past experiences with them, this could allow your struggle to remain.

A key part of healing is in renouncing all homosexual involvement and asking God by His Spirit to cut the cords and dig out the roots that would bind your soul with another. This should be done with every sexual relationship experienced prior to your marriage.

Deliverance is something we all need at some time in our lives. It is God's intervention to free us from whatever controls us. We have to cooperate with Him in the process, which sometimes includes standing against demonic spirits. Second Corinthians 10:4 says, "The weapons we fight with are not the weapons of the world. On the contrary, they have divine power to demolish strongholds." And in Ephesians 6:12 we read, "For our struggle is not against flesh and blood, but against the rulers, against the authorities, against the powers of this dark world and against the spiritual forces of evil in the heavenly realms."

We are in a spiritual battle, but we are promised victory if we stand in the authority of God's Word. This is a daily process and, in one sense, deliverance is living every day with the assurance that we do not have to serve sin. We can speak to that "pull" toward the past, and break its power. The struggle will get easier.

Q. I am not a lesbian any longer. I have been married for many years, but I am afraid to form a close bond with another woman. Does this mean I have demons, or that I'm really not straight?

A. I think the fear of close friendships can come from unresolved hurts or rejections from the past. It can be a tool of Satan to hold your memory in bondage to forgiven behavior. If you have repented of homosexual relationships, and God has forgiven you, which He does when we ask, then you are not homosexual.

The friendships you develop must be built on mutual respect and nondependent interaction. I recommend reading Lori Thorkelson's booklet *Emotional Dependency*. It will clarify what dependency relationships are and how to avoid them. Then pray for some special women friends to come into your life, and grow together.

No, this doesn't mean you have demons or that you are not straight. You should pursue healing of the spirit, and would benefit from books on inner healing of memories mentioned in Appendix IV.

Q. I've been through healing of memories sessions and some deliverance, but I never felt anything worked completely. I still have temptations. Should I go through it again?

A. A misconception of inner healing and deliverance is that they are something that someone does for you once, and you are magically well with never another temptation or wrong sexual feeling. Healing is more like peeling an onion. Layer by layer our protective shell is removed, and sometimes we cry. We didn't receive all of our hurts in life at one time, and the healing process can take years. We need not live, however, as victims of the past. We can choose to walk in freedom each day, building new experiences and allowing redemptive love to bring healing. You will never be without temptation. But you will be able to mature in Christ to the point where you are no longer obligated to serve those temptations.

Daily Freedom

Q. How do I let go of yesterday and just live for today? What if I fall again?

A. People hold onto past memories for a number of reasons. Sometimes because they felt accepted, special and happy when relationships were new. Sometimes because they are afraid of the future and of developing new friendships. In one sense, remembering the past is good. You can remember what you were without Christ. To live for today is to know that you are forgiven the sins of the past, and have sufficient strength to do God's will today.

The fear of falling into sin tomorrow will keep you paralyzed. Memorize 1 Corinthians 10:13: "No temptation has seized you except what is common to man. And God is faithful; he will not let you be tempted beyond what you can bear. But when you are tempted, he will also provide a way out so that you can stand up under it."

Carry that verse with you and read it daily until it is chiseled into your memory.

Forgiveness

Q. When I was a child, my dad would get drunk and force me to have sex with him. I hated him. When I was a teenager I became a Christian and now I think my dad had a demon controlling him. I still hate him even though he is dead. How can I forgive him?

A. Only the grace of God can enable you to do what you haven't the strength to do on your own. Forgiveness is a choice we make based upon the Bible's command to forgive. Anger is a valid emotion when an adult betrays the trust of a child and victimizes her. God can bring healing to that little girl and take away the poison of hatred. Your father is dead but he lives inside your memory, and in order for you to move along on your journey, you should find a trusted counselor and work through this issue. You might also benefit from *A Door of Hope* by Jan Frank.

Q. I know God's Word says that He forgives us when we confess our sin. I know this in my mind, but in my heart I feel Satan telling me I can never be forgiven for the bad things I've done. Can you help me?

A. There is a verse written especially to Christians that applies here. It is 1 John 1:9: "If we confess our sins, he is faithful and just and will forgive us our sins and purify us from all unrighteousness." Also applicable is 1 John 3:19–20: "This then is how we know that we belong to the truth, and how we set our hearts at rest in his presence whenever our hearts condemn us. For God is greater than our hearts, and he knows everything."

The Bible says that Satan is a liar and a thief, so when he comes to steal your peace and confidence in what God has done for you, call him a liar and thank God for the forgiveness and purity He is working in your life.

Depression

Q. I can't tell anyone else. I am so depressed. I think of suicide all the time. Do you ever feel helpless and lost?

A. Depression can come from both emotional and physical causes. First, I recommend a complete medical checkup to confirm that nothing physical is causing the depression.

If nothing physical turns up, then perhaps seeing a Christian counselor would be beneficial to help you sort out why you are experiencing these feelings. Counselors can often provide an alternate viewpoint. Suicide is never God's answer to depression.

Sometimes something as simple as getting involved in a Bible study or taking a walk or some other physical activity will help depression.

The helpless and lost feelings might have roots in not being in control of your life. Take a close look at what you are doing, what your goals are and how you are working to achieve them.

If your depression is caused by regrets in your life about past experiences, then you need to turn each memory over to God, forgive the individuals involved and receive His forgiveness. You must live only one day at a time.

I have also learned in the times I feel helpless to call a friend and talk about the issues. I find strength in mutual prayer. It will work for you, too.

Causes of Homosexuality

Q. There is so much debate as to the causes of homosexuality. Science is trying to prove it's genetic. What do you believe?

A. I believe that, despite a host of contributing factors (none of them genetic), homosexuality is not God's intent for mankind, and that through Jesus Christ He has made complete provision for healing of both the behavior and the orientation. I believe that Scripture establishes a firm foundation of sexual responsibility prior to marriage, which is abstinence. That applies to everyone.

The reason homosexuals want to find a hormonal or genetic basis for homosexuality is to establish a legitimate minority status for those who choose to identify with the gay community.

The Bible states in Genesis 1:27: "So God created man in his own image, in the image of God he created him; male and female he created them." Homosexuality was not an option at creation, and is not a viable alternative now.

Q. Can you explain the fact that I've had these feelings all my life?

A. Most of the recent psychological research indicates that the roots of homosexuality extend into not only early childhood, but as far back as infancy. There was often some detachment or failure to bond with a parent, which set up the situation of emotional brokenness. Simply because you cannot remember ever feeling different doesn't support the theory that you were born gay.

Often parental expectations of children force them to assume roles in which they are not comfortable. One man, Bruce, tells of his father's insistence that he become involved in football, because "real men like sports." His brother was very physical and enjoyed outdoor activities Bruce enjoyed spending time with his mother and practicing the piano. Before he was ten, he was labeled a sissy.

The environment plays a significant part in the homosexual's brokenness. but the causes are diverse. Current understanding is not the "domineering mother/absent father" syndrome, but a combination of factors that include an emotional detachment from the same-sex parent. Elizabeth Moberly, the psychotherapist from England, has done the most extensive and believable research and writing in this area. Her book is in the recommended reading section.

A more important point to consider here is that regardless of the cause, the Bible calls it sin. Christ died for our sins, and that includes homosexuality. It is not the worst sin, but it is a difficult process to work through for complete healing, even after the sin is forgiven. Jesus is not baffled at its complexity, but has promised healing and freedom to all who will choose to follow Him and be obedient to the teachings of His Word.

Q. When I was ten, I was molested by our youth minister. Doesn't that mean that even then there was something that drew him to choose me instead of the other boys? I came from a non-Christian home, and I thought that church was a place where people would really love me.

A. Your story is like so many from men who were seduced or raped by those who were entrusted with their care. It is especially sad that it was a youth minister, because we should be able to trust Christians. It does not mean, moreover, that anything was wrong with you. The problem was with the minister, and he probably felt there was no place he could go and find help. Case studies tell us that persons who were molested as children have a high instance of molesting children when they become adults.

Also, a Christian environment can be a perfect set-up for these perpetrators because of the affection and trust of children. Many pedophiles seek such an environment because of the trust that has been instilled in children to be nice to Mr. So-and-So. This is a tragic situation, and parents in any environment should always be on the lookout for suspicious behavior. In your situation, coming from a home where your parents were not with you in church, you were a likely target. You were looking for friends, for love and acceptance, and responded when special caring was directed toward you.

If you have not already done so, you should seek professional counseling regarding the abuse issue and the homosexual involvement. Again, you were not to blame for what the youth minister did. It was his brokenness. Eventually you will be able to forgive him and move ahead in your healing. You must not blame Christianity for the actions of those who are its representatives. All of us have imperfections and are prone to sin without the grace of God to transform our lives. Keep your eyes on Jesus, and learn of His full acceptance and love toward you.

Homosexual Friends

Q. I have been gay for more than ten years. All my friends and most of my business associates are homosexual. Do I really have to give up my gay friends to live a Christian life?

A. Although leaving them behind is probably the most difficult thing to do, it is certain that if you try to live in both worlds you will fail. The influence of the gay lifestyle will pull you back into relationships that will hinder Christian growth.

I have found that as you begin to attend a church, establish yourself in a Bible study support group and change your behavior, the old friends will tire of hearing about Jesus. You won't have to offend them by cutting them out of your life. As you grow in Christ, they will have less and less in common with you.

It is important to realize, too, that attending gay functions, hanging out in gay clubs and perhaps continuing to wear the fashion styles of the gay community will keep you all too connected. You must choose to make changes, if you want to avoid temptation. This will also involve books, pictures and other remnants of a homosexual lifestyle. It could involve a change of employment, moving to a new residence or even to another state if that's what it takes to keep you free from homosexual involvements.

You should work at establishing new friendships with Christian men and women who are committed to serving God.

Q. I was in a Christian drug rehabilitation center when I accepted Christ. I thought I could make it when I left there and returned to my old neighborhood. In a few weeks, I backslid. What can I do to get right with God and live as He wants me to? I'm not doing drugs now, but my ex-lover keeps coming over, and it's hard to tell her to leave.

A. The first thing to do is confess your sinful activity, ask God to forgive you and determine never to give in to that sin again (1 John 1:9).

Then you need to find a new support system, which

may include leaving your old neighborhood. Check in with the Christian drug center for suggestions. You need to find new friends and a loving, supportive church fellowship to help you mature as a Christian.

When your ex-lover comes around, tell her straight out that Jesus is your Savior and that you are not going to sin with her again because the Bible says it is wrong. You need to plan ways *not* to be at home if you know she is coming over. If she comes to your home without warning, tell her you have plans to go somewhere and can't stay with her. Then go. (Keep a plan sheet of places to go, so that you are not telling her a lie.) This will be hard at first, but she will get the message.

Make a firm decision to maintain your relationship with Jesus *at any cost*. He will assist you in making positive choices to avoid friendships that will hinder your growth. You cannot cut out old friends without replacing them with new. This is an ongoing step in Christian maturity.

Steps to Healing

Q. I have a friend who used to be gay. He loaned me your book *Long Road to Love*. I just recently became a Christian but struggle with thoughts of the past. How long will it take me to get healed, and do I need inner healing?

A. Healing for persons with sexual addictions and brokenness is an ongoing process that may take years. The sense of struggle will diminish as the time goes by, but there will always be areas of your life that God is healing as you mature in Him.

If you make the decision to break from the lifestyle, find a church or support group. Find people with whom you can be honest about your struggle, and who will accept you in the struggle and prayerfully support you. Establish a personal Bible study and prayer time. Break all ties with the past, as God reveals relationships that will hinder your growth. With all this, you will just be starting your journey of healing.

It will probably be a year before you feel you have made any progress, but every day of choices will be another stone in the foundation of wholeness.

I recommend starting and maintaining a journal during this time. It will remind you of victories, and encourage you when you feel setbacks in your emotional struggle.

I believe all of us have areas of brokenness that are within our souls and can be mended only by the Spirit of God. This healing need not be a marathon of specific prayer healing with a group, but often it is helpful to have someone pray with you who is sensitive to the Spirit's leading. If there are areas that surface or memories of abuse (sexual, emotional or physical), these are inner wounds that need Jesus' touch. It is important to understand that God takes the sting out of these memories, but that scars will remain. You will not forget the event happened, but you can move beyond its crippling effect in your life.

I emphasize the word *process*. You will grow as you learn what God's Word teaches and determine to live accordingly each and every day.

Loneliness

Q. I attend church and have quit seeing my gay friends. I am so lonely that I sometimes contemplate suicide It's hard to believe that God is with me during these times. How can I overcome these feelings?

A. First, it is important to realize that for single people, there is always going to be a certain feeling of "aloneness." In Genesis 2:18 we read, "The Lord God said, 'It is not good for the man to be alone. I will make a helper suitable for him.' "

This does not mean that everyone should expect to get married, but it tells us that as human beings we are created to interact with other people. We do not function well in isolation.

One step to overcoming loneliness is to become involved in your church fellowship. Perhaps a singles group there offers activities. You do not have to focus in on special friendships, but should begin to establish several casual friendships. Then, if one person is busy, you will have the option of doing something with one of the others in the group.

If you have any hobbies or areas of special interest, you might pursue classes as a method of establishing new friendships.

You can volunteer at places like rest homes, shelters or city projects. Visiting the AIDS wards or any other shut-ins is another way to keep your life from becoming too lonely. It will also give you less time to think about your past.

Hebrews 13:5–6 says, "Keep your lives free from the love of money and be content with what you have, because God has said, 'Never will I leave you; never will I forsake you.' So we say with confidence, 'The Lord is my helper; I will not be afraid. What can man do to me?' "

God's Word says He is with you always . . . and He will not abandon you. The loneliness that paralyzes will pass as you ask Him for creative ways to reach out to others.

Gay Spouses

Q. I have known for some time that my husband is gay. I don't want to leave him, but have received counsel that I could get a divorce on biblical grounds. Do you think he will change if I stay committed to the marriage?

A. This is not an easy question because you don't provide background information.

If your husband is trying to deal with his homosexual behavior, then you would benefit from support groups or material that addresses this issue. Referrals are available from Exodus.

If he is not interested in change, then you have a different situation. If there are children involved, it becomes complicated even further.

I would say that even marriages that are terminated on biblical grounds leave scars that may take years to heal, for both parties. If there is a chance of staying committed to the marriage and working things through, then you should give it every chance.

I know of one marriage that went through twelve years of struggle as the husband fell into sexual sin on a regular basis. His wife loved him and prayed for him. Each time, he would repent and vow it would never happen again. It did.

They both sought counseling and she refused to give up on her husband or the Lord's ability to change him. The pain was incredible. He finally received therapy for the root causes of his homosexuality and they have been growing together in Christ for the past seven years with no sexual setbacks.

It doesn't always happen, but it is possible to work out the marriage if you stay committed to God . . . and to the marriage.

Q. Two years ago my wife left me to live with her best friend. I know they are involved in a lesbian relationship. We are both Christians and I cannot understand how she could abandon our marriage. What makes a woman become a lesbian when she was straight for so many years?

A. First of all, being a Christian doesn't insulate you from the sinfulness in the world. It doesn't guarantee that you will not become involved in personal sin.

Secondly, your wife didn't just turn into a lesbian and leave you on the spur of the moment. She apparently had some deep issues in her life that were not resolved.

One of the possibilities is that she was a victim of sexual abuse as a child and never found healing. You don't say how long you were married, but it's possible that marriage just brought all the feelings to the surface, and she didn't know how to deal with them.

One couple I know had this experience. When the wife wanted to talk about being sexually abused and about her teenage involvement with all types of sexual behavior, her husband would have none of it. He is a minister and said, "What God has forgiven, He forgets. We should do the same."

Each time she called me, it was because there was no communication in their marriage. She continues to be filled with issues that have no resolution since he won't support her in any therapy because of his ministry position. This is a marriage with a time bomb that will explode someday.

It is seldom a sexual experience that women seek initially as they draw closer to other women, but rather the intimacy that may be lacking in a marriage. The sexual involvement happens in a progression of steps that the women may not even be aware of at first.

You mentioned that you were both Christians, so I would recommend you continue to pray for her and, if you have the opportunity, encourage her to find a group where she can talk about the issues that got her involved in this relationship.

Don't give up on her, or God. He can restore your marriage.

Q. My husband had homosexual encounters prior to our marriage. He says he isn't fooling around now, but I'm not sure. Should I continue having sexual relations with him? How do I treat his friends some of whom, I suspect, are his lovers?

A. If your husband's known encounters were within the past ten years, you should encourage him to take an AIDS test, if he has not already done so. A marriage is built on a foundation of trust, and you might express your concerns without accusation and listen to his explanation. If he has special friends with whom you suspect he is sexually active, you could confront him directly after praying for wisdom; you could insist on the use of condoms when you have intercourse; and you might suggest counseling.

Your fears may not be justified, and the developing of close male friendships can be a sign of healing of his former homosexual condition.

Get to know his friends, and treat them as you would anyone else. If there is a sexual relationship involved, it won't be hidden for long.

Q. I think my husband is gay, but I'm not sure. Can I tell for sure?

A. Generally, no. There are "signs" you might look for, but they can be misleading. Again, if any marriage is to survive, there must be a foundation of trust and an openness of communication. You cannot tell by how a man looks, or even acts, whether or not he is struggling with homosexual identity. If he expresses concerns in this area, you should encourage him to talk to a Christian counselor or contact an ex-gay mninistry for support.

Q. My ex-husband is gay. When should I tell our children? What do I say?

A. Your children should be told when they are at a level of understanding that will not produce unreasonable fears. If he is in an active relationship with someone, you might want to establish guidelines for visitation. Children should be given a biblical presentation of homosexuality on their level of comprehension. They should be encouraged to pray for their dad and be affirmed in their love for him. Each case is different, and wisdom should be exercised in providing information to young children.

Christian and Gay?

Q. I met a woman recently who is a lesbian and confesses Christ as her Savior. Can you be gay and a Christian?

A. There are many Christians who deal with issues of sin in their lives. There are Christians who commit adultery, watch pornography and engage in many types of sexual involvement, including homosexuality.

But the person who has a personal relationship with Jesus Christ, who accepts the Bible as the inspired Word of God and wants to live by its principles, cannot choose to sin.

First John 2:1–6 states,

> My dear children, I write this to you so that you will not sin. But if anybody does sin, we have one who speaks to the Father in our defense—Jesus Christ, the Righteous One. He is the atoning sacrifice for our sins, and not only for ours but also for the sins of the whole world. We know that we have come to know him if we obey his commands. The man who says, "I know him," but does not do what he commands is a liar, and the truth is not in him. But if anyone obeys his word, God's love is truly made complete in him. This is how we know we are in him: Whoever claims to live in him must walk as Jesus did.

You can be a Christian, and realize that your behavior does not match up with God's standard. You should try to change the behavior, not the standard! The process of changing outward behavior begins by experiencing the inner healing of the heart that will transform the soul.

Attempting to transform behavior without a deeper healing will always result in a return to the sinful behavior and a frustration with being unable to "make the Bible work for me."

I do not believe a person can be a committed Christian, with all that it implies, and be a committed lesbian or gay man.

A close investigation of a person who claims to be Christian and gay will reveal that he or she usually accepts only a limited scope of biblical teaching.

The attitude of the heart for the Christian who struggles with sin will be one of seeking healing and deliverance from the things that separate him from the fullness and fellowship of Christ.

AIDS-Related Questions

Q. My ex-husband is HIV-positive. Can my children get AIDS from Daddy's kisses? Should I be concerned about his seducing our boys?

A. While the AIDS virus is present in low concentrations in saliva, there is no known instance of its being passed through kissing. Generally there is no reason to believe that because your ex-husband has an adult male relationship, he would try to involve your sons in sexual activity. If he has had pedophile tendencies then you might want to establish supervised visits.

Q. My daughter is gay. Is it true that lesbians do not get AIDS?

A. No, this is not true. Gay men are most at risk in being infected with the HIV virus, but it can be transmitted between women also. Any time body fluids (including saliva and tears) come in contact with breaks in the skin, someone is at risk of infection.

While lesbians have not had a high percentage of infection in the past, the numbers are increasing with the monthly AIDS statistics. Anyone who engages in sexual activity with multiple partners places herself at risk.

Q. I am a gay man and I have never taken the AIDS test. I have decided to remain celibate. My family doesn't know about my homosexual activity, and I don't want to tell them now. Since I am in my early twenties, how can I explain to them that I am never going to date or get married?

A. First of all, I encourage you to reconsider your position on not taking the AIDS test. If you have had sexual contacts since 1980, you are in a high-risk group. You will never know if you had exposure to the AIDS virus without a blood test. You may appear healthy and still have the AIDS antibodies in your system.

I can understand your fear about not wanting to tell your family, but if you did come down with ARC or AIDS, they would be entitled to know for their own protection.

Also, you are a young man, and even though marriage seems like a non-option at this point, I would encourage you not to limit God. If you have not committed your life to Christ, I would encourage you to do so.

There are ex-gay groups around the country that can provide support as you deal with the issues of homosexuality. I would encourage you to contact ARM in Santa Monica to find out more about AIDS. Perhaps you will be able to draw support from others who have struggled with whether or not to take the test.

You will live with greater fear by not knowing if you have the virus, than if you found out for sure. The researchers say that some drugs like AZT will be more effective in the earlier stages of the disease than after it has progressed.

Do not let fear rob you of responsible behavior to others and to yourself. You will have much to thank God for if you are not infected with the virus.

There is healing available from the brokenness that has occurred due to your homosexual involvement. I encourage you to gain support from others who have overcome their homosexuality. Perhaps one day you will be free to share that victory with your parents.

The questions will never end. The book must. If you wish to contact me, please do so.

Darlene Bogle
P.O. Box 3504
Hayward, CA 94540
(415) 785–0349

Appendix II

Glossary of Terms

Acquired Immune Deficiency Syndrome (AIDS)

An acquired defect in the immune system function that reduces the affected person's resistance to certain types of infections and cancers. It is caused by a virus (HIV or HTLV III) that is transmitted through intimate sexual contact or exposure to infected blood or blood products. Once immune deficient, a person with AIDS becomes susceptible to a number of opportunistic diseases.

AIDS Dementia Complex (ADC)

A neuropsychological disorder created by the AIDS virus itself or an AIDS-related opportunistic infection. Damage to the brain varies. It can range from an alteration of the brain's metabolism to actual tissue damage. Symptoms include forgetfulness, difficulty in concentrating, impaired judgment, personality changes and weakened motor skills.

AIDS Related Complex (ARC)

This is a name some scientists use to describe physical conditions that are generally less severe than fully developed AIDS. It is sometimes called Pre-AIDS; however, people do die with ARC without ever developing full-blown AIDS.

AZT

A drug known as Azidothymidine that is used to treat certain groups of AIDS patients. It seems to prolong survival of some patients. It is available to anyone who has recovered from PCP.

Bisexual

A male or female person who enjoys sexual activity with the same or opposite sex equally.

Full-Blown AIDS

A term used to refer to a person who has come down with specific diseases identified with the AIDS virus. It is only when this diagnosis is given that it is reported to the Centers for Disease Control.

Gay

The accepted terminology to describe both a member and the lifestyle of the homosexual community. This term came into common usage in 1979 at the riots of the Stonewall Club in New York. It was that event that caused the homosexual community to band together in marches around the country to demand gay rights.

Gay Bars

Hangouts for the gay community. Most are designated preference, either all-male or all-female clientele.

Heterosexual

A male or female attracted to the opposite sex. Does not have to engage in sexual activity to be heterosexual.

HIV

This is the proper name for the AIDS virus. In 1984 scientists at the National Cancer Institute were able to identify the cause of AIDS as one of the "human retroviruses." They found a specific one called human T-lymphotropic virus type III or, more simply, HTLV-III. At the same time in France there was found a similar virus, lymphadenopathy associated virus or LAV. An international committee of scientists decided to call the virus human immunodeficiency virus (HIV).

Homophobia

Irrational fear of homosexuals. Many times ascribed to anyone in the straight or Christian population who takes a stand against homosexuality.

Homosexual

A male or female attracted to the same sex. Does not have to engage in same-sex activity to assume the label of homosexual. Some believe the orientation to same-sex relationships is what classifies someone as homosexual, while others hold that behavior is the key factor.

Kaposi's Sarcoma (KS)

A tumor on the walls of blood vessels. Usually appears as pink-to-purple painless spots on the skin, but may also occur internally. Death occurs from major organ involvement.

Lesbian

A female homosexual. (Also called butch, dyke or femme.)

Opportunistic Diseases

Those diseases that are caused by agents that are frequently present in our bodies or environment, but which cause disease only when there is an alteration from normal, healthy conditions, such as when the immune system becomes depressed or destroyed.

Pneumocystis Carinii Pneumonia (PCP)

A lung infection seen in immuno-suppressed people. It is caused by protozoan present almost everywhere, but is normally destroyed by healthy immune systems. Once a person develops PCP he is susceptible to recurrence of the disease and the outcome may be fatal.

Straight

Any heterosexual.

T-Cells

White blood cells that are processed in the thymus. They produce lymphokines and are responsible, in part, for carrying out the immune response of the body. They are also called T-lymphocytes.

Turning Tricks

A term for paid sexual encounters. Commonly used with reference to male prostitutes.

Virus

A tiny, submicroscopic living parasite that invades cells and alters their chemistry so that the cells are compelled to produce more virus particles. Viruses cause many infectious diseases. They can reproduce only in living cells.

Appendix III

Support Groups/ Hotline Numbers

Support Groups (Christian)

Exodus International
P.O. Box 2121
San Rafael, CA 94912
(415) 454–1017
(Keeps a current listing of all ex-gay ministries and AIDS support groups.)

ARM
AIDS Resource Ministries
1415 3rd St. Promenade #201
Santa Monica, CA 90401
(213) 395–9137
(Offers support groups for parents and for those who are HIV-positive or have AIDS.)

Spatula Ministries
P.O. Box 444
La Habra, CA 90631
(213) 691–7369
(A group for parents. Founded by Barbara Johnson.)

Support Groups (Secular)

FLAG (Friends of Lesbians And Gays)
P.O. Box 27605
Washington, D.C. 20038
Attn: Brochures
(202) 638–4200
(A parent group.)

MAP (Mothers of AIDS Patients)
c/o Barbara Peabody
3403 E St.
San Diego, CA 92102
(619) 234–3432

National Coalition of Gay Sexually Transmitted Disease
Services
c/o Mark Behar
P.O. Box 239
Milwaukee, WI 53201
(414) 277–7671

San Francisco AIDS Foundation
333 Valencia St., 4th Floor
San Francisco, CA 94103
(415) 863–2437

U.S. Public Health Service
Public Affairs Office
Hubert H. Humphrey Building, Room 725–H
200 Independence Ave., S.W.
Washington, D.C. 20201
(202) 245–6867
(For the Surgeon General's Report on AIDS.)

AIDS Education Office
1730 D St., N.W.
Washington, D.C. 20006
(202) 737–8300
(Information on local or American Red Cross.)

Toll-Free Hotlines

Public Health Service AIDS Hotline
1–800–342–AIDS (342–2437)

National Sexually Transmitted Disease Hotline
American Social Health Association
1–800–227–8922

National Gay Task Force AIDS Information Hotline
1–800–221–7044
In New York: (212) 807–6016

Daily Statistics on AIDS

Centers for Disease Control
1600 Clifton, N.E.
Atlanta, GA 30333
(404) 330–3020 or 3021

Appendix IV

Recommended Reading

AIDS

How Will I Tell My Mother?
Jerry Arterburn
Oliver Nelson Publishers, 1988

Power in the Blood:
   A Christian Response to AIDS
David Chilton
Wolgemuth & Hyatt Publishers, Inc., 1987

You Can Protect Yourself and Your Family from AIDS
Clif Cartland
Fleming H. Revell Co., 1987

Christian Counseling

Called to Counsel
Dr. Timothy Foster
Oliver Nelson Publishers, 1986

Counseling the Homosexual
Michael R. Saia
Bethany House Publishers, 1988

Getting Them Sober:
A Guide for Those Living with Alcoholics
Toby R. Drews
Bridge Publishing, Inc.
Vol. 1, 1980
Vol. 2, 1983
Vol. 3, 1986

Homosexuality: A New Christian Ethic
Elizabeth Moberly
James Clarke, Cambridge, 1983

Unmasking Satan
Richard Mayhue
Victor Books, 1988

Development of Homosexuality

The Broken Image:
Restoring Personal WholenessThrough Healing Prayer
Leanne Payne
Crossway Books, 1981

Crisis in Masculinity
Leanne Payne
Crossway Books, 1985

Emotional Dependency:
A Threat to Close Friendships
Lori Thorkelson
Exodus International
Available through Regeneration Books, Baltimore, Md.

The Homosexual Person:
    New Thinking in Pastoral Care
John F. Harvey, O.S.F.S.
Ignatius Press, 1987

Long Road to Love:
    A True Story of Hope for the Homosexual
Darlene Bogle
Chosen Books, 1985

Overcoming Homosexuality
Ed Hurst with Dave and Neta Jackson
David C. Cook Publishing Co., 1987

Parents of the Homosexual
David and Shirley Switzer
The Westminster Press, 1980

Sex Roles and the Christian Family
W. Peter Blitchington, Ph.D.
Tyndale House, 1980

Steps Out of Homosexuality
Frank Worthen
Love in Action

Where Does a Mother Go to Resign?
Barbara Johnson
Bethany House Publishers, 1979

You Don't Have to Be Gay
J.A. Konrad
Pacific Publishing House, 1987

Spiritual Healing

Bonding:
    Relationships in the Image of God
Donald M. Joy, Ph.D.
Word Books, 1985

A Door of Hope
Recognizing and Resolving the Pains of Your Past
Jan Frank
Here's Life Publishers, 1987

Healing for Damaged Emotions
David A. Seamands
Victor Books, 1981

Healing of Memories
David A. Seamands
Victor Books, 1985

Inner Healing through Healing of Memories
Betty Tapscott
Hunter Publishing Co., 1971

Making Peace with Your Inner Child
Rita Bennett
Fleming H. Revell Co., 1987

The Power to Heal
Francis MacNutt
Ave Maria Press, 1977

Pursuing Sexual Wholeness:
How Jesus Heals the Homosexual
Andrew Comiskey
Creation House, 1989

Rebonding
Donald M. Joy, Ph.D
Word Books, 1987

General

Beyond Rejection
Don Baker
Multnomah Press, 1985

Strangers in a Christian Land

The Hurting Parent
Margie and Gregg Lewis
Zondervan Publishing House, 1988

Living with Your Passions:
    A Christian's Guide to Sexual Purity
Erwin W. Lutzer
Victor Books, 1984

Love Must Be Tough
James Dobson
Word Books, 1986

Parents in Pain
John White
InterVarsity Press, 1979

Special Ministries for Caring Churches
Robert E. Korth, Editor
Standard Publishing Co., 1986

What Every Family Should Know About Homosexuality:
    Growing Up Straight
Dr. George A. Rekers
Moody Press, 1982

When Parents Cry
Joy P. Gage
Accent Books, 1980

When Going to Pieces Holds You Together
William A. Miller
Augsburg Publishing House, 1976

These books and many others relating to human sexuality
    are available through:

Regeneration Books
P.O. Box 9830
Baltimore, MD 21284

Write for a catalog.